Peter Stadelmann

Tropical Fish

Setting Up and Taking Care of Aquariums Made Easy

Expert Advice for New Aquarists

With color photographs;
illustrations by Fritz W. Köhler

Consulting Editor:
Matthew M. Vriends, PhD

BARRON'S

Contents

Preface

Full of expectations of a beautifully designed underwater world with opalescent fish and gorgeous water plants, the novice aquarist starts to set up his tank. Often, however, the beginner's pleasure soon turns to disappointment: the fish and the plants are in dire straits, and no one seems to know just why. Usually, fundamental errors have been made, errors that easily can be avoided—and this *Complete Pet Owner's Manual* will help you do so.

Author Peter Stadelmann explains, in a way anyone can follow easily, the essentials of setting up and taking care of an aquarium. On how-to pages, with the help of graphic drawings, he tells step by step how to set up the tank, from the bottom material to the aquarium equipment. In addition, he suggests what plants to buy and includes many tips on taking care of the aquarium and plants and feeding the fish.

With concrete suggestions about good combinations of fish and descriptions of fish suitable for beginners, he answers the aquarist's most vital questions: "Which fish and how many of them?" and "Which fish are well suited to each other?" To equip the aquarist to deal with out-of-the-ordinary events, there are two helpful tables: "Emergency Aid for Breakdowns in the Aquarium" and "The Most Common Diseases of Fish and Their Treatment."

Precise directions, brilliant color photographs, and informative drawings make this book an indispensable companion for all new aquarists.

Looking at an aquarium is relaxing and exciting at the same time. The green of the plants provides a restful counterbalance to the splendid play of the fish's colors and their interesting patterns of behavior. Most aquarists enjoy their idle hours in front of the aquarium.

To keep your pleasure in your hobby untarnished, please pay heed to the note of warning on page 63.

Buying and Equipping an Aquarium

F ish are among the oldest living vertebrates. They originated in the Silurian period, at least 430 million years ago. Present-day freshwater species evolved only 60 million years ago, in the Tertiary period. By comparison human beings—with their approximately 40,000-year history—are newcomers on earth.

In setting up a freshwater aquarium, you are creating a habitat for fascinating, splendidly colored fish from tropical waters. To provide these exotic beauties with the appropriate environment, you will need technical accessories and tools for their care. Everything required for operating an aquarium as a hobby is available in pet stores.

The Right Aquarium

The first step toward becoming an aquarist is the acquisition of a suitable aquarium. Although at first glance all aquariums look alike—apart from their size—there are differences in quality. When buying an aquarium, don't be penny-wise and pound-foolish. Good brand-name aquariums will last a long time and save you a good deal of trouble, unlike many economy models. So-called all-glass aquariums, available with or without frames, are customary today.

The right size: I know scarcely any aquarists who started off in a big way when they first took up their hobby. Most people want to see first how things go, and therefore start small. The tank should not be too small, however; after all, an aquarium must be a suitable habitat for many plants and fish. For this reason I recommend the standard tanks, between 24 and 63 inches (60–130 cm) long (see Aquarium Dimensions and Volume, table, page 7).

Lighting

The fish kept in a freshwater aquarium come from countries where the light conditions are quite different from those in most parts of the United States. The light there is more intense moreover, its brightness remains approximately the same for 12 to 14 hours at a stretch. For this reason there is no way you can avoid using artificial light.

Aquarium lighting: The simplest solution is to buy an aquarium cover with one or more holders for fluorescent tubes. They are available for all aquariums with standard dimensions. Fluorescent tubes use little energy but yield good light and radiate almost no heat. The number of tubes needed depends on the depth of the water. For a 24-inch (60-cm) tank with water about 12 inches (30-cm) deep, one tube is sufficient, while two are needed in a 39-inch (100-cm) tank with a water level of about 16 inches (40-cm).

Light color: When buying tubes, pay attention to the color of the light, which is designated by numerals. Colors appropriate for an aquarium are marked 11, 21, and 41. I recommend 41, because its warm tone makes the colors of the fish and plants especially attractive.

Period of illumination: From 12 to 14 hours continuously, without fail. Interruptions harm the plants, which become stunted. In addition, algae problems develop. To ensure that the light is turned on and off punctually, install a time switch.

boy feeding his fish. The two angelfish (Pterophyllum scalare) are already waiting.

Heating

In regulating the water temperature, just as in providing light, take into account the conditions in the tropical native waters of your fish. For the fish described in this book the temperature must be between about 75 and 79° F (24–26° C) continually.

A heater with automatic control will ensure that the temperature in the aquarium remains constant. Simplest to operate are automatic heaters with the temperature marked on the adjusting knob. All you need to do is select the desired temperature, for example, 75° F (24° C). The water temperature then will hover between 75 and 77° F (24–25° C). Greater precision is not required, because slight variations in temperature do not harm the fish. Attach the heater in one of the back corners of the aquarium.

A pair of swordtails. In contrast to the female (above), the full-grown male (below) normally has a pointed, elongated tail fin.

My suggestion: As an alternative to an automatically controlled heater, you may use heating cable, which should be laid in coils and kept in place with cable anchors on the bottom pane of the aquarium. Do not kink the cable. Your pet store owner can advise you.

Filters

To keep your aquarium clean and your fish healthy, a filter is essential. It will remove waste products such as fish excrement, food remnants, or decomposing plant parts from the water and recondition it. There are various types of filters. I recommend inside or outside filters driven by a rotary, or centrifugal, pump.

Inside filter: Attach the filter in one of the rear corners. It has a limited effect and therefore should be used only in small tanks. In large tanks it is useful as ancillary equipment—for example, to produce a stronger water current.

Outside filter: Place the outside filter next to the aquarium or on the aquarium stand. It can be used for both small and large tanks. This filter often marketed incorrectly as a suction filter. For practical instructions on filter installation see page 18.

My suggestion: A thermal filter is very practical. In it the aquarium water is first cleaned, then brought to the correct temperature. One enormous advantage is that you need no extra cable and hence lose no space in the aquarium.

Filter materials: Macroporous expanded plastic is used for the inside filter (filter cartridge). A coarse filter substrate goes in the outside filter. Filtering charcoal is suitable for "follow up treatment" when medication is administered (see page 60). A number of other filtering materials are used for various purposes or in large filters (small clay pipes, for example). I advise against the use of cotton wadding as a filter because it compresses too quickly (except in combination with charcoal filtration).

Aquarium Dimensions (in inches) and Volume (in gallons)

Length	Width	Height	Volume
24	12	12	14
32	14	15	29
39	16	16	42
39	16	20	53
47	16	20	63
51	16	20	69

Bottom Material

The bottom covering in an aquarium has two functions. First, it is the medium in which the roots of the plants take hold and which stores nutrients for them. Second, it serves as an element of the aquarium's decoration and design.

Quartz gravel with a grain size of 3 to 5 millimeters is an ideal bottom covering. Larger grain sizes are less well suited, because the gravel would pick up too much dirt and is too hard to keep clean. Pet stores carry pre-washed gravel, which nevertheless has to be washed again before it goes into the aquarium. Gravel must be neutral—that is, free from lime—so that the water conditions are not affected. It also should not be too light in color, or it will reflect too much light.

Sand has disadvantages: it decays easily, and plants do not grow well in it. However, for some fish—such as *Corydoras* and barbs, which like to root in the bottom—you may add a small patch of sand.

A nutritive substrate supplies the aquarium plants with vital substances. Add it to the gravel in the form of a long-lasting fertilizer when you set up the aquarium, or press it in tablet form into the gravel at some later time.

Decorative Materials

Stones and roots are the most important decorative objects in an aquarium. You can use them to create an appropriate environment and provide the hiding places that some fish need (for example, fish that establish a territory, such as cichlids or red-tailed black sharks). Decoration really is a matter of individual taste.

Stones: Suitable for this purpose are all primary rocks—for example, quartz; granite; red, green, and black slate; and lava that is free from lime (not sharp-edged; if necessary, break the edges with a few hammer blows).

Roots: You can use oak roots from marshlands (do not take live roots out of the ground) or so-called marsh pine roots. Just don't use roots that come fresh from the woods.

Ceramic and fired-clay caves make the best hiding places and nesting holes.

Backdrop: There are backings with various motifs that can be glued to the pane from outside.

What doesn't belong in an aquarium: The fish can injure themselves on sharp-edged objects. The following have an unfavorable effect on the water: roots that come fresh from the woods, stones that contain lime, seashells, and coconut shells.

For many fish a root in the aquarium is a favorite hideaway.

Other Accessories

A thermometer is absolutely essential to control the water temperature. A simple aquarium thermometer is sufficient. Attach it to the pane with a suction cup, opposite the automatic heater.

Time switches are highly recommended so that you can keep the period of "daylight" constant (12 to 14 hours per day). Thus you are in no danger of forgetting to turn the light on or off.

The brilliantly colored varieties of guppies are among the most popular aquarium fish.

CO₂ fertilizing devices promote the growth of the plants. I recommend a spray chamber or a CO_2 diffuser. These devices, inexpensive and easy to use, keep carbon dioxide (CO_2) "on tap." Systems that provide a constant supply of carbon dioxide are not recommended for the beginner, because improper operation can result in an overdose. For a 24-inch (60-cm) tank you need one device; for a 30-inch (100-cm) tank, two are required. They can be arranged side by side (diffusers) or mounted one upon the other (chambers) without difficulty.

Debris vacuums are practical for cleaning the bottom material.

An algae magnet or a pane scraper will make cleaning easier.

An oxidizer is a special device that can be used to add oxygen to the water. It does not need to use electrical current and is quite helpful if you need an immediate remedy when breakdowns occur or the fish fall ill.

An aquarium stand that serves as a base is advisable for large, heavy aquariums. Such a stand is suited by virtue of its design to carry large loads In addition, you can keep the outside filter and accessories on it.

Tips for Making Your Purchase

• Important in making all decisions that relate to your aquarium: take your time. First, get the aquarium and all the accessories. It is very important to: Se up the aquarium first, then buy the fish three—or, even better, ten—days later. The water needs time to develop into a habitat suitable for fish (see What Happens during the Waiting Period, page 16).

• When in doubt, have someone explain to you how the equipment works.

Like a painting: A variety of guppy with a particularly striking tail fin.

• Don't buy the plants for your aquarium indiscriminately. A plan like those shown on pages 14 and 19 will ensure that you can create a varied layout in your aquarium. An unbalanced selection of plants with little variety of species can have bad results (see Waste Products in the Aquarium, page 46).

The Right Location

Thanks to modern equipment that provides sufficient light inside an aquarium, any place in your home can be used. Keep the following points in mind, however:

• You should be able to gaze at your aquarium in comfort—perhaps from your favorite armchair.
• There must be enough room available for you to perform comfortably all the tasks necessary to take care of your aquarium.

• At least one electrical outlet should be available near the aquarium.
• For a 24-inch (60-cm) aquarium a sturdy table makes an adequate base. To test its sturdiness, first sit down on it yourself. Larger aquariums are best placed on a special aquarium stand.

Not suitable as locations are window sills (it is too bright and hot there in the summer) and all other places where the aquarium cannot remain year-round.

Safety around the Aquarium

Water damage and insurance: The nightmare of many aquarists—that their aquarium will burst—becomes reality relatively seldom. Nonetheless, you should be prepared for such an eventuality. Water damage, which incidentally can also be caused by an overflow or development of a leak in

About the photos:
It is no wonder that the rapidly multiplying guppy is also known as the "million fish." There is scarcely an aquarist who did not begin his career with these brightly colored fish, which are easy to take care of.

9

the aquarium, usually involves very high repair costs. Even before you buy your aquarium, have it added to your household goods insurance and ask your insurance agent what expenses are covered.

Protection against electrical accidents: Various electrical appliances such as filters, heaters, and lights are necessary to create proper living conditions for fish and plants in an aquarium. It is well known that electricity can be dangerous when it comes into contact with water. Consequently, give close attention to the following suggestions for safety:

• When buying electrical appliances, purchase only Underwriters Laboratory (UL) approved equipment. Electrical equipment in the aquarium must state that it can be safely used under water.

• Obtain a so-called fault current protective switch (available in pet stores and electrical supply stores), which can be attached between the current source and the appliance. In case of defects in the appliances or cables, it will interrupt the power supply at once.

• Pull the plug before you do any work in the aquarium or remove electrical appliances from the aquarium.

• If repairs are necessary, have them performed by a professional.

Shopping List for a 25-Inch (60 cm) Aquarium

You can get all the following basic equipment at the same time. Then, wait three to 10 days before purchasing the food and fish.

One all-glass aquarium, 24 x 12 x 12 inches (60 x 30 x 30 cm), with or without a frame.
One styrofoam sheet 10 millimeters thick (only if your aquarium has no frame).
Six bags of gravel weighing 5½ pounds (2.5 kg) each, with a grain diameter of 3 millimeters, not too light in color.
One package of nutrient substrate.
Three pebbles or slate stones.
One flat pebble or piece of slate.
One aquarium root.
A water conditioning agent.
One liquid fertilizer for subsequent care of plants.

One rotary-pump inside filter with an expanded plastic filler.
One automatically controlled heater (50 W) with a degree scale.
One aquarium cover with a built-in fluorescent tube (15 W), color 41.
One backdrop.
One aquarium thermometer.
One pane scraper (algae magnet).
One hose for changing the water, about 5 feet (1.5 m) long and 12 to 16 millimeters thick.
One bucket, 2.6-gallon capacity (10 L), to be used solely for the aquarium (label it!).
One time switch for the lights.
Possibly 1 multiple plug.
And don't forget the plants (see pages 14 and 19)

Setting Up the Aquarium–Step by Step

Before You Begin

A weekend or a vacation day will be just right for setting up your new aquarium. It takes a fair amount of time. Nothing is more annoying than having to empty an aquarium that has just been set up because you've made a mistake in your haste to get the job done.

Preliminary Work

Before you get started a few chores are necessary.
- Leave the aquarium plants in their packing until you are ready to set them, or put them in a bowl with some water in it (keep them in a dark place). Plants that wilt will not recover.
- Twenty-four hours before the appointed time, put the aquarium root in a bucket of hot water and scrub it until all the bark is removed.
- To check whether the tank has survived the trip home and is water-tight, place it carefully on a level surface (your balcony or cellar floor) and fill it with water. Any leaks will show up quickly.
- After this test, wash out the tank with lukewarm water.
- Wash the gravel thoroughly: fill a bucket one-quarter full with gravel, let water run over it, and stir the gravel with a small hand shovel. Keep pouring out the dirty water and refilling the bucket with clean water until the water is almost completely clear. When you pour the dirty water into the drain, hold a large colander underneath so that gravel will not plug the drain.

- Using water and a brush, clean the rocks.
    Important: Do not use detergents; the residue can impair the water quality. Lukewarm water is quite sufficient.

The Proper Aquarium Water

Tap water to which a water-conditioning agent has been added is fine for the initial filling of the aquarium. The aquarium first has to be "broken in" with the filter, heater, and lights on, and during this phase the water will develop in the correct way. Only very hard tap water (see Water Hardness, page 43) needs further conditioning (ask your pet store dealer).

If You Have Bought the Fish and the Aquarium at the Same Time

If you introduce fish into an aquarium that has not been broken in, they will not feel at ease and will have difficulty becoming acclimated. Their health can be so seriously impaired that they may die in a short time or waste away over a period of weeks. In addition, the biological processes that are crucial for a healthy aquarium start operating only very slowly. What do you do, however, if—contrary to all good advice—you have bought the fish and the aquarium at the same time, or, as frequently happens, friends beaming with joy come to inaugurate your aquarium, bearing a bag of fish? Then only an emergency aid program will help (see page 17).

An aquarium thermometer is absolutely indispensable in controlling the water temperature.

11

False loosestrife (Ludwigia repens).

Fanwort (Cabomba aquatica).

Cabomba piauhyensis.

Cryptocoryne wendtii.

Water plantain with cordate leaves.

A water plantain blossom.

Indian water frond.

Plants perform many functions in an aquarium. They help maintain the water by producing oxygen and making use of organic waste products. They provide hiding places for the fish and serve as spawning sites. Not least, they are beautiful.

Vallisneria gigantea.

Anubias barteri.

13

How-To Setting Up the Aquarium

The following pages provide directions for setting up a 24-inch (60-cm) tank. The materials needed to do so are listed on page 10. If you want a larger tank (39 inches = 53 gallons, or 100 cm = 200 L), you will find further tips for setting one up and suggestions for plants on pages 17 through 19.

Setting Up the Tank and Putting In the Bottom Covering
Illustration 1

Put the aquarium in its permanent location (see The Right Location, page 9). Tanks that lack frames should be set on a styrofoam base; those with frames must be placed directly on the platform! Spread two bags of gravel over the bottom of the tank, sprinkle the nutrient powder on top and add the remaining bags of gravel.

Decorating and Pouring In Water
Illustration 2

Build a cave in the tank with rocks. Make a circle with three rocks, press firmly into the gravel, and lay flatter stone on top. On the opposite side stick the root into the bottom material.

Fill the tank about one-third full with water. First, set a saucer on the gravel and put a bucket of lukewarm water next to the aquarium. The water level in the bucket should be higher than the level you intend to have in the aquarium. Fill a hose about 5 feet (1.5 m) long with water

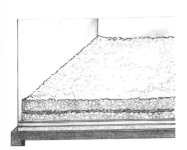

1 Put in the gravel and nutrient powder (as a ground fertilizer).

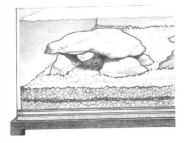

2 Build a cave and put a root opposite it.

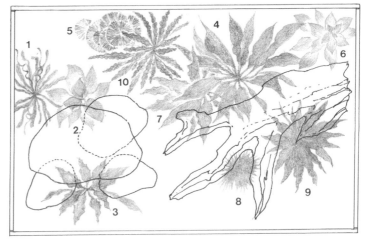

3 Suggestion for setting plants in a 24-inch (60-cm) tank.

The plants (one bunch or pot of each):
1. Corkscrew vallisneria. (Vallisneria spiralis).
2. Anubias barteri.
3. Cryptocoryne wendtii.
4. Black Amazon (Echinodorus parviflorus).

5. Fanwort (Cabomba aquatica), two bunches.
6. False loosestrife (Ludwigia repens).
7. Swordfern (Microsorium pteropus).
8. Liliaeopsis novae zelandiae.
9. Cryptocoryne walkerii.
10. Echinodorus osiris.

at a water faucet or in a filled sink. Hold your thumbs over both ends of the hose. Put one end into the water in the bucket, the other on the saucer. Remove your thumbs, and the water will flow into the tank; direct at the saucer at all times so that the bottom covering is not disturbed. To stop the flow close the end of the hose in the bucket with your thumb.

Placement of the Plants
Illustration 3

This illustration shows one way you might arrange your plants decoratively.

Setting the Plants
Illustration 4

Stem plants: The leaves of these plants are located so far apart that you can see the stem, or stalk, between them. Lay the plant flat on the gravel and weight it with a pebble. Anchored in this fashion, the plant will put forth roots at several axillae simultaneously and strike root very quickly.

Rosette plants: These plants, which have leaves arranged in the shape of a rosette, are often sold in little baskets with rock wool. To take them out turn the basket over, hit it against a table edge, and loosen the plant from its container. Using scissors, cut the roots to a length of about 1 inch (3 cm).

Then use your finger to bore a hole in the gravel, and put the plant in it so that the very top of the root remains free. Then refill the hole.

My suggestion: Tie swordfern to the aquarium root with Perlon thread.

Installing Appliances
Illustration 5

Before you attach the filter and automatic heater, slowly fill the tank with water to a level about ¾ inch (2 cm) below the upper edge, while adding the water conditioning agent bit by bit. If any plants have been washed out inadvertently, reset them.

Using the suction cups provided, install the filter in the left rear corner and the heater in the right rear corner. In accordance with the marking, attach the suction cups of the heater to the top third of the device. Fix the thermometer on the left part of the aquarium's front pane. Using adhesive tape, fasten the backdrop to the outside of the aquarium's rear pane. Carefully lower the cover with the fluorescent tube onto the aquarium. Plug in the appliances and turn on the light and the time switch.

Important: Delay the introduction of the fish until the cloudiness of the water has disappeared (see page 16).

4 Weight stem plant with a stone. For rosette plants dig a hole and set the plant so that the very top of the root is left free.

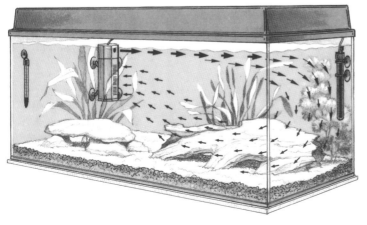

5 A completed aquarium with an expanded plastic inside filter (left rear), a heater with automatic control (right rear), and a thermometer (left front).

As you can see, kissing gouramis are aptly named.

What Happens during the Waiting Period

The completed tank must, as I have said, be "broken in" for a time. Let the filter and heater run, set the timer for the aquarium lighting for a cycle of 12 to 14 hours (from 8 A.M. to 10 P.M., for instance), and don't put in a single fish while the water is still cloudy. For the sake of the fish, wait patiently. Even without fish you will have much to gaze at over the next few days. The water will appear cloudy, even brownish at times. It will be full of little air bubbles, and a whitish slime may appear on the panes. These signs are entirely normal. Subsequent developments will show you how the water becomes a suitable habitat for fish.

The cloudiness of the water is caused by the deposit of fertilizer as it dissolves. Later the cloudiness will be removed gradually by the plants and,

in part, by the filter. Introduce the fish only after the water has cleared!

Brownish water frequently is caused by the roots placed in the tank as decoration. Roots give off humic acid, which gives the water a brownish tint. It is not harmful, and the coloration will disappear almost entirely with regular changes of water.

The white slime on the panes is a colony of bacteria that feed on free protein in the water. Later this slime will be eaten by snails or removed when the panes are cleaned. It is not necessary to clean the panes as a precautionary measure at this stage.

Aid Program for Fish Introduced Too Soon

If you have introduced your fish too soon and notice that they are not feeling well, take the following measures:

1. Every three days change one-

't is fascinating to watch... *the gouramis' lively courtship.*

hird of the water and add some of the conditioning agent.

2. Test whether the filter is still letting enough water through. If it is only trickling, clean the filter (Filter Maintenance, page 49).

3. Give food only in flake form, and little of it. Add vitamins to the aquarium water.

4. Do not fertilize the aquarium plants until the tank is broken in.

5. After about two weeks, the aquarium will have "calmed down." Now is the time to switch to a normal rhythm of maintenance (Aquarium Care Made Easy, pages 43 to 54).

6. Add new fish only after two more weeks.

Tips for Decorating a 39-Inch (100-cm) Tank

A larger tank will have room for a second cave built of stones, for example.

In addition, you can arrange the bottom material to form steps. In combination with the plants, such a "terrace" is very decorative in appearance.

Here's how to construct the terrace: Build the terrace in the rear half of the tank. It can be created with the help of slate stones: Put one or more slate stones into the empty tank about 4 to 6 inches (10–15 cm) from the rear pane. The gravel should be deeper behind the slate than in front of it.

Installing an Outside Filter

At first glance installation of an outside filter seems quite complicated. If you follow the sequence of steps outlined here, however, and keep an eye on a few things, the filter will work on the first try. Proceed in this way:

● Attach the filter hoses to the filter housing.

About the photos:
Kissing gouramis (Helostoma temminckii) during courtship. For these fish, which are classified as labyrinth fish, kissing is one component of a lively courtship. If you look closely, you can make out the rasping teeth (to scrape off algae) behind the thick lips.

• Open the filter housing and pour the filter mass between the strainers. (Don't add the substrate still packed in little bags, and don't use cotton wadding as a filter.)

• Dampen the gasket, place the motor head with the gasket on the filter, and tighten it.

• Connect the filter to the intake pipe (if at all possible, by means of couplings).

• Briefly suck at the return hose, using either your mouth or a mechanical aspirator, in order to start water flowing into the filter housing. The filter housing will fill slowly with water.

• Connect the return hose to the nozzle pipe. The nozzle pipe should be attached below water level. Adjust the nozzles so that the stream of water flows horizontally from the rear toward the front pane.

• Wait until the rising water has forced the air out of the filter into the return hose. When the gurgling has stopped, the air is out.

• Now plug it in. The filter will run at once. Any hissing sounds that it makes now are caused by air escaping from the new filter material. If the motor chatters, pull the plug, then plug it in once more.

Important: Never turn the filter off, except for maintenance procedures.

Decorating with Plants

If you don't use the suggestions for plants on pages 14 and 19 or if you want to redecorate your aquarium later, keep the following fundamentals in mind when selecting and arranging the plants:

• The plants' environmental needs should be more or less in keeping with the requirements of your fish.

• Find out all you can about the growth potential of the plants you want. In small tanks you will have to keep cutting back plants that grow too large, and in the long run this will not agree with them.

• Plants that form a carpet belong in the foreground, while those that grow taller ought to be placed on the sides or in the background. A highly decorative specimen (single plant) can also enliven the middle ground. Be careful to place the plants so as to leave the fish enough swimming area.

These Plants Are Suitable for a 39-Inch (100-cm) Tank (see illustration, above)

1. *Cryptocoryne nevillii*, ten bunches
2. *Echinodorus grisebachii*, ten pots
3. *Aponogeton crispus* or *Aponogeton ulvaceus*, two plants.
4. Red tiger lotus (*Nymphaea zenkeri*), one plant.
5. *Anubias barteri* var. *nana*, three pots.

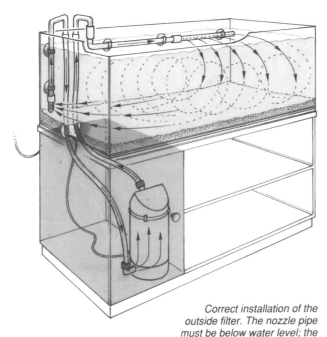

Correct installation of the outside filter. The nozzle pipe must be below water level; the nozzles point toward the front.

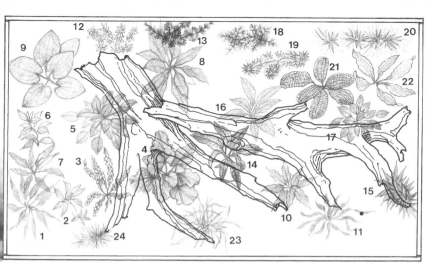

Suggestion for setting plants in a 39-inch (100 cm) tank.

6. Argentinian waterweed *(Egeria densa)*, three plants, free-floating.

7. *Cryptocoryne walkeri*, three bunches or pots.

8. Black Amazon swordplant (*Echinodorus parviflorus*), three pots.

9. Swordplant, or elephant ear (*Echinodorus cordifolius*), one pot.

10. *Cryptocoryne wendtii*, three pots.

11. *Cryptocoryne balansae*, one bunch.

12. Loosestrife (*Rotala rotundifolia*), three bunches.

13. Water purslane (*Didiplis diandra*), three bunches.

14. Swordfern (*Microsorium pteropus*), two pots.

15. *Nomaphila stricta*, three pots.

16. *Anubias barteri* var. *barteri*, two pots.

17. *Anubias barteri* var. *nana* (dwarf variety), three pots.

18. Water wisteria (*Hygrophila difformis*), three bunches.

19. Waterweed, or pondweed (*Egeria densa*), five bunches.

20. *Vallisneria gigantea*, two plants.

21, 22. *Echinodorus osiris*, two pots.

23. Arrowhead, or needle sagittaria (*Sagittaria subulata* var. *pusilla*), five bunches.

24. *Lilaeopsis novae zelandiae*, three pots.

As pretty an aquarium landscape as can be created. The fish feel at home in this lovingly and generously designed tank. The photo shows a community of South American fish, including large angelfish and various characins.

Selecting and Buying the Fish

B efore you buy fish, get the equipment and set up the aquarium. It takes a while for a newly completed aquarium to develop into a habitat suitable for fish. For a tropical freshwater aquarium you need, besides the tank, lighting, a heater, a filter, decorative materials, and other accessories.

Selecting the Right Fish

The wider the choice, the harder the decision. The supply of fish available is so diverse and enticing that new aquarists have a hard time limiting themselves and putting together a balanced community. Overpopulated tanks, with animals that are under stress and prone to bouts of disease, are the result.

Correct association: Fish cannot be placed together haphazardly. There are rowdy fish that make life difficult for the peace-loving ones, and playful fish that nip at everything that swims across their path and make no exception of beautiful long fins. The fish must be suited to each other not only in behavior, but also with respect to the water quality and temperature they require. In the suggestions for stocking an aquarium, on page 23, you will find exemplary communities of fish. Additional reference points are given on pages 27 through 38.

If you put together your fish community on your own, note the following:
• Many fish have preferred habitats. Some like to stay near the surface of the water, others prefer the middle strata, and still others keep close to the bottom. Find out all you can about the living habits of the fish you want, and make your selection so that every area of the tank is occupied.
• The widespread rule "¼ inch (1 cm) of length for every 1½ to 2 quarts (1.5–2 L) of water" should be followed with caution. Thirty cardinal tetras, for example, are just over 1 inch (3 cm)

long when fully grown, but they require fully as much room as one pair of kribs (*Pelvicachromis pulcher*). The amount of excrement produced—that is, the waste disposal problem—is identical in both cases.
• Find out exactly what the living requirements of the individual fish species are (see The Most Popular Fishes for Beginners, pages 27–28, and Suggestions for Further Reading, page 63).
• Don't introduce all the fish simultaneously; put them in the tank in relatively small lots (see Buying the Fish, page 24).

Where to Get Fish

Pet stores offer a large selection of fish throughout the year. As a rule, you will find well-trained personnel there, able to help with all problems and to advise you.

Friends who have young fish to give away, for example, or who would like to change their community of fish should be used as a source only if their aquariums are clean and well maintained and if the water conditions correspond with those in your aquarium. Fish have low tolerance for a change in water quality.

Latin Names of Fish

Since the Swedish naturalist Carl Linné introduced the so-called binomial system of nomenclature (designation with two names), every living being—whether animal or

Suggestions for Stocking a 24 x 12 x 12 Inch (60 x 30 x 30 cm) Aquarium

	3 to 10 days after tank is set up	After 10 more days	After 4 more weeks
Suggestion 1:	3 flying foxes 1 bristle-mouth catfish	7 neon tetras 5 black phantom tetras (2 males, 3 females) 5 harlequin rasboras 2 dwarf gouramis (1 pair) 3 corydoras	4 guppies or 4 platies (2 pairs)
Surface fish: rasbora.			
Suggestion 2:	3 flying foxes 1 bristle-mouth catfish *Inhabits the middle strata of the tank: Sumatra barb.*	7 zebra danios 5 Sumatra barbs 3 half-striped barbs 3 corydoras 2 kribs (1 pair)	4 platies or 4 black mollies (2 pairs)
Suggestion 3:	3 flying foxes 1 bristle-mouth catfish	7 zebra danios 5 black tetras 3 corydoras	4 platies (2 pairs) 4 guppies (2 pairs) 2 black mollies (1 pair)
Suggestion 4:	3 flying foxes 1 bristle-mouth catfish	7 *Hyphessobrycon herbertaxelrodi* 5 rosy tetras or red phantom tetras 3 corydoras	3 Siamese fighting fish (1 male, 2 females) or 2 butterfly fish

Suggestions for Stocking a 39 x 16 x 20 Inch (100 x 40 x 50 cm) Aquarium

Suggestion 1:	4 to 6 flying foxes 1 bristle-mouth catfish	25 neon tetras or cardinal tetras 7 bleeding heart tetras 5 Congo tetras 1 red-tailed black shark 7 moss green Sumatra barbs 10 corydoras	6 butterfly fish (3 pairs) or 2 kribs (1 pair) After 2 more weeks: 3 angelfish
Suggestion 2:	4 to 6 flying foxes 1 bristle-mouth catfish	25 rasboras 10 emperor tetras 10 Boehlke's penguin fish 3 clown loaches 4 snakeskin gouramis (2 pairs) 10 corydoras	6 butterfly fish (3 pairs) After 2 more weeks: 3 angelfish
Bottom dweller: corydoras.			

Siamese fighting fish—a shimmering blaze of colors.

plant—has been classified in the following way. The first name gives the genus to which a living being belongs. The second name designates the species within the genus. The cardinal tetra, for example, bears the Latin name *Paracheirodon axelrodi*. The purpose of this nomenclature is to prevent confusion worldwide, because different languages use widely disparate common names for the same fish. It is important that you remember the Latin name or mention it when buying a fish, even though fish keep being renamed. The cardinal tetra used to have the Latin name *Cheirodon axelrodi*. Most pet store dealers, however, know both the new and the old names.

Buying the Fish

For an aquarium that has been newly set up, buy the fish in several lots in succession. After the breaking-in period (three to ten days, depending on tank size), algae eaters like flying foxes or bristle-mouth catfish should

This red variety of Siamese fighting fish is an impressive figure in an aquarium.

be first in line, as a cleaning team. Introduce the rest of the fish in two lots, at intervals of 10 to 14 days.

My suggestion: Cautious aquarists keep newly purchased fish in quarantine for about four weeks. The quarantine tank should be set up just as completely as the community tank, but should contain no other fish.

Tips for buying fish:

• Buy fish only from well-maintained aquariums (clear water, clean panes, no dead fish in the water).

• Don't hesitate to buy young fish, even if they are smaller and paler.

• Don't buy at peak shopping hours. The salesperson will have more time to advise you, and it will be less stressful for the fish.

• Watch for possible symptoms of disease, such as white, granular spots; cottony, white patches; frayed fins; or dull skin (see page 55).

• Come to the tank frequently and watch how the fish behave as the days pass. Healthy fish swim about in a

25

lively manner and are not shy. It would be a good idea to stay on hand at feeding time and watch the fish eat. Healthy ones eat swiftly.

Transport

The pet store dealer will pack the fish in a plastic bag half full of water. For insulation a layer of newspaper is wrapped around it. Take the quickest way home. The trip will place the animals under great stress, and the shorter the journey, the better. Take care to keep the bag horizontal so that the fish have more swimming area. In addition, the larger water surface will allow more oxygen to enter the water.

Introducing the Fish into the Aquarium

Fish are poikilothermic animals, whose body temperature adjusts to the outside temperature. They tolerate changes in temperature poorly. Therefore, do not put them in the tank at once. First, place the sealed bag in the water. Wait until the water temperature in the carrying bag conforms to that in the aquarium. You must wait at least 15 minutes for this to happen.

Now open the bag and slowly mix the carrying water with the aquarium water. Pour aquarium water into the bag until it is full. Finally, tip the bag and let the fish swim free.

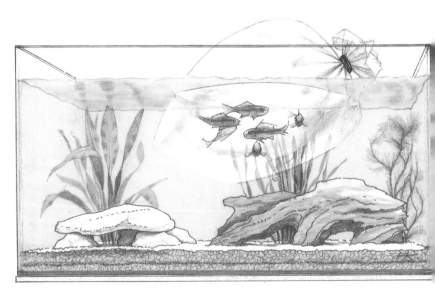

Putting in the fish. Let the closed carrying bag rest in the water for a while, until the temperature in the bag conforms with that of the water.

The Most Popular Fish for Beginners

In this chapter, I will present a small selection of fish that are particularly easy to take care of. They can easily be kept in a community tank at an average temperature of 75 to 79° F (24–26° C) and a pH of 6.5 to 7.5. More precise information is supplied where necessary under the heading "Care." You will learn something about each family and somewhat more about various species. In addition, there are tips about which fish get along well with which others. The sizes given are average values for fish kept in an aquarium; in their natural habitat fish grow larger.

Explanation of the Headings

Care: Here you will be given information on the special needs of the fishes in regard to tank size and decoration. The measurements in inches refer to the length of the aquarium.

Food: Normally dry food is adequate as a basic nutrient. Many fish, however, appreciate special treats.

Special tips on recommended species: Here you will learn how many fish of any species should be put in your tank (a school or pairs), and you will become acquainted with interesting modes of behavior peculiar to each species.

Live-bearing Toothed Carp
Family *Poeciliidae*

The live-bearing toothed carp are among the most popular aquarium fish. Almost every "old hand" among aquarists began his career with them, because the species and varieties of this family are pretty and robust, and they spawn readily. Characteristic for this group is the astonishing fact that these fishes bear live young. In the male the anal fin is transformed into a special copulative organ, called the gonopodium. During mating it is inserted into the genital opening of the female, and insemination occurs. Part of the sperm fertilizes the eggs that have developed inside the female, and part can be stored by the female for later series of ova. The young develop in the eggs inside the mother until, at birth, they burst through the egg membranes and enter the water as fry.

Care: In tanks of at least 24 inches (60 cm). Sides and rear lightly planted, leaving ample free swimming area. Partial covering of water surface with floating plants. Do not have soft, acid water in the tank; hence do not put in too many roots or any peat extracts. The pH should exceed 7. If you want to raise the young, scoop them from the water surface with a very fine-meshed net and transfer them to a spawning tank (available in pet stores). Otherwise they will be eaten by larger fish. Relatively large spawning tanks are also suitable places to put the mother before spawning, so that the young can be born there.

Food: Various kinds of flaked foods. Mosquito larvae (frozen) must be given in addition. The fry need special pulverized flakes.

Argentine waterweed (Egeria densa) is a good contributor of oxygen. It needs frequent trimming.

27

Black molly (Poecilia sphenops).

Swordtails (Xiphophorus helleri).

Zebra danios (Brachydanio rerio).

Paradise fish (Macropodus opercularis).

Red-tailed black shark (Labeo bicolor).

Flying fox (Epalzeorhynchus kallopterus).

Platies (Xiphophorus maculatus).

These photographs show popular aquarium fish that are easy for a beginner to deal with. The black molly, swordtail and platies are live-bearing toothed carp; the zebra danios and flying foxes are barbs; the red-tailed black shark and clown loaches are classified among the loaches and other *Cypriniformes*.

Clown loaches (Botia macracantha).

Special Tips on Recommended Species of Live-bearing Toothed Carp

Guppy (*Poecilia reticulata*); see photos on title page and pages 8 and 9; male, 1 to 1½ inches (3–4 cm) long; female, up to almost 2½ inches (6 cm) long. Many varieties somewhat larger. Vigorous swimmer, prefers small groups (four to six members of the same species). The males harry the females constantly, so keep more females than males if possible. Long-tailed species have a tendency to fin rot and fungus infections. Do not keep these kinds together with fish that nip fins (the Sumatra barb, for instance), otherwise the slow-moving guppy males will suffer.

Green or Mexican swordtail (*Xiphophorus helleri*); see photo on page 28: 2 to 3 inches (5–7 cm) long. The males in particular are lively and temperamental. One often sees several males trying to impress each other. As in the case of the guppy, the males often harry the females quite intensively, so try to have the females outnumber the males (for example, two males with four to six females in a 39-inch [100 cm] tank). A handy eradicator of algae.

Platy (*Xiphophorus maculatus*); see photo on page 29: Males, ¾ to 1 inch (2–3 cm) long; females, 1 to 1½ inches (3–4 cm) long. A lively fish, it likes to live in small groups (five to seven fish). It will pull algae off decorations and plants.

Requires similar care: Variegated platy (*Xiphophorus variatus*). The platy and the swordtail are closely related. If they interbreed, surprising color variations will result. This fish prefers a tank with a dark bottom—with sand-stones—that is densely planted with various types of vegetation.

Black molly (*Poecilia sphenops*); see photo on page 28. A lively fish

about 1½ to 2½ inches (4–6 cm) long, it likes to live in a small group (four to six members of the same species) and combs the entire aquarium for algae. It spawns readily. The black molly is sensitive to extremely soft water and to pH values under 7.

Requires similar care: Sailfin molly (*Poecilia velifera*); 2 to 3 inches (5–7 cm long; useful as an algae eater.

Labyrinth Fish
Suborder *Anabantoidei*

The labyrinth organ of a labyrinth fish. By means of this organ the fish can breathe in air even above water level. The air inhaled is pressed into this organ, and the oxygen is drawn from it there.

These brightly colored fish owe their name to a specialized organ in the area behind their head, the labyrinth organ (see illustration at left). It enables these fish, which generally live in oxygen-depleted waters, to inhale atmospheric oxygen as well. Because of their long, thread-like ventral fins, they also are called threadfish.

Their method of reproduction is worthy of note. The males of most species build fairly compact nests of foam at the water surface (see illustration, page 31). They take air bubbles from the surface of the tank into their mouth, surround them with a sticky secretion of foam, and finally spit them onto the water surface. Soon a veritable castle of foam towers up there. In it the eggs are laid, and it is the male that watches over them until they hatch. You can easily keep these fish in pairs.

Care: They can be kept in a 24-inch (60-cm) tank, but one at least 32 inches (80 cm) long is preferable. It should be densely planted around the sides, with a partial cover of floating plants. Avoid strong currents. Because labyrinth fish—with the exception of the paradise fish, or macropodes (*Macropodus opercularis*)—love warmth, the lower temperature limit should be 77° F (25° C).

Food: Dry food, with frozen live food for variety.

Special Tips on Recommended Species of Labyrinth Fish

Dwarf gourami (*Colisa lalia*); see photos on pages 36, 37, and 56. An even-tempered fish about 1½ inches (4 cm) long, which usually stays in the upper part of the tank or wanders among the rocks and plants. It should be placed together only with small, school-forming fish or bottom dwellers that do not nip at the long threads of the ventral fins. The males are brightly colored, while the females are paler and less distinctly patterned.

Requires similar care: The exceedingly beautiful honey gourami (*Colisa chuna*), ¾ to 1 inch (2–3 cm) long. Should not associate with extremely lively fish.

Blue, golden, opaline, or snakeskin gourami (*Trichogaster trichopterus*); see photo on page 57; up to 4 inches (10 cm) long. A very robust species that can hold its own against fish of equal size in a community tank. Tank must be at least 32 inches (80 cm) long.

Requires similar care: Kissing gourami (*Helostoma teminckii*); see photos on pages 16 and 17; 4 inches (10 cm) long; needs a tank at least 39 inches (1 m) long. Pearl gourami (*Trichogaster leeri*); 4 inches (10 cm) long; should not associate with lively fish such as Sumatra barbs.

Paradise fish, or macropode (*Macropodus opercularis*); see photo on page 28. The most robust of the labyrinth fish, about 2½ to 3 inches (6–8 cm) long. Needs a tank at least 32 inches (80 cm) long. May be a troublemaker, annoying other ornamental fishes, if they are very slow. Keep only one pair in a 32-inch (80-cm) tank. The females have shorter fins, are not nearly as brilliantly colored, and are slightly plumper than the males.

Siamese fighting fish (*Betta splendens*); see photos on pages 24 and 25; About 3 inches (7 cm) long. As the name indicates, they are fighting fish—only the males, however—and are very aggressive with one another. Consequently, keep only one male in your tank. Keep several females along with the male, because a lone female often will be hunted. Fighting fish are peaceable toward other inhabitants of the tank, however, unless they have similar fin veils. They do well in a community tank.

A male paradise fish builds a foam nest, in which the eggs will be laid later.

Barbs and Other Cyprinids
Order *Cypriniformes*

Barbs owe their name to the short, thread-like beards, or barbels (Latin: *barba* = beard) that many have as organs of touch to the left and right of their mouth and sometimes on their lips as well. Owing to their gorgeous coloring and agility, they enliven the tank tremendously. Do not keep smaller species together with the more robust larger species, otherwise the smaller ones will suffer.

F ish communicate with each other by means of scent and movement, by changing their color patterns, and even by making sounds. Many aquarium fish make noises so loud that they are audible to the human ear. They sound like growls, squeals, or clicks. The paradise fish, for example, occasionally makes a perceptible loud smacking noise.

Care: In tanks at least 24 inches (60 cm) long; densely planted around the sides and partial shade from floating plants. Barbs need a great deal of room for swimming. A relatively dark bottom covering and roots will accentuate the beauty of these fish. They have a sensitive reaction to pH values above 7.5. A pH of 6.5 would be ideal.

Food: All the customary types of foods.

Special Tips on Recommended Species of Barbs

Harlequin fish, or red rasbora (*Rasbora heteromorpha*); see photo on page 41. A school-forming fish about 1 inch (2.5 cm) long, it shows to advantage only in a group of seven to ten. A cheerful, peaceable fish, it should not be kept together with larger fish that travel in schools if they are too abrupt in their behavior. The pH should not exceed 7.

Requires similar care: The false harlequin barb (*Rasbora hengeli*); about 1 inch (2.5 cm) long.

Sumatra tiger barb (*Puntius tetrazona*). About 1½ inches (4 cm) long. This fish travels in schools, and in a troop of five to seven animals the largest male "calls the tune." A vivacious, robust species, in motion all day long. Not suitable for association with peaceable small fish or with fish that move slowly and have long fins (angelfishes, gouramis); sumatra barbs constantly nip at their fins.

Require similar care: Some varieties—for instance, the moss-green Sumatra barb. (see photo on page 41).

Zebra danio (*Brachydanio rerio*); see photo on pages 28 and 29: A large, spirited, school-forming fish, just over 1 inch (3 cm) in length, which feels at ease only in a relatively large school (seven to eight fish, preferably more). Likes to spend time just under the surface of water that is open and bright. Ideal for association with all other fish, with the exception of peaceable surface dwellers. The species also will spawn in a community tank. If a carpet of floating plants covers a small portion of the water surface, some fry also come to the top. In this way they are able to avoid persecution by other inhabitants of the tank.

Half-striped, or banded, barb (*Puntius semifasciolatus var.*); see photo on page 40. An active, school-forming fish about 2 inches (5 cm) long that should be kept in small groups (four to six animals). The species spends its time near the bottom, ceaselessly searching for food. An ideal associate for fishes that do not need too much peace and quiet.

Require similar care: Cherry barb (*Puntius titteya*); about 2¼ inches (5.5 cm) long; somewhat harder to please, not so lively. Black ruby or purple-headed barb (*Puntius nigrofasciatus*); about 2 to 2½ inches (5–6 cm) long; males have far more intense coloring than females. It likes a large tank with a dark bottom; plants such as *Cryptocoryne* are recommended.

Flying fox (*Epalzeorhynchus kallopterus*); see photo on page 29. This species, about 3 to 4 inches (7–10 cm) in length, should be kept in a tank at least 32 inches (80 cm) long. Flying foxes need shelter in the form of roots, which protect them while they take a rest. Otherwise, they are not fussy. Major destroyers of algae. The fry are gregarious, but with increasing age they become territorial and slightly aggressive toward each other.

A pair of angelfish (Pterophyllum scalare) ➤ *with a clutch of eggs. Angelfish pair off naturally, and a pair often will mate for life. The partners choose a corner of the aquarium as their territory and defend it.*

Requires similar care: Siamese flying fox (*Epalzeorhynchus siamensis*), about 3 to 5½ inches (7–14 cm) long.

Catfish
Order *Siluriformes*

Catfish, found worldwide, live in waters of all depths. Over the course of their phylogeny they have been quite adaptable and have occupied extremely diverse ecological niches. In an aquarium catfish generally make themselves useful at "garbage disposal," because—depending on the species—they clean up algae and food remnants.

Care: In tanks at least 24 inches (60 cm) long. Provide some shade with floating plants. Include roots and stone caves as shelters. Keep the area near the bottom open.

Food: Omnivorous.

A black-bellied upside-down catfish searches a root for something to eat.

Special Tips on Recommended Species of Catfish

Bronze or Aeneus catfish (*Corydoras aeneus*); see photo on page 45. About 3 inches (7.5 cm) long. A bottom dweller, it likes to travel in a group (three to five fish) and scours the tank bottom for anything edible. For routine feeding, use tablets.

Require similar care: Peppered corydoras (*Corydoras paleatus*); about 2 inches (5 cm) long. Dwarf corydoras (*Corydoras cochui*); just over 1 inch (3 cm) long; always should be kept in a school.

Black-bellied, or African, upside-down catfish (*Synodontis nigriventis*), About 3 inches (7 cm) long. Three to five animals in tanks at least 32 inches (80 cm) long. They need several shelters, which usually are shared by only two fish. As the name indicates, it swims on its back. It feeds—unusual for catfish—under the water surface.

Blue bristle-mouth, bristle-nose, or blue-chin catfish (*Ancistrus species* aff. *dolichopterus*). Males may grow as long as 4¾ inches (12 cm), while females are smaller (this applies to this species only; other *Ancistrus* types may reach almost 8 inches [20 cm]). The most efficient window-cleaner (algae eater) in the aquarium. A loner, it needs its own cave, which it defends against intruders. Outside the cave, however, it is extremely peaceable. The males develop an imposing head decoration composed of branched "antennas," or bristles.

Cichlids
Family *Cichlidae*

Cichlids are the fish "with character" in the community tank. They occupy territories, and many species pair for life. They routinely spawn in a community tank. The fry receive devoted care and are defended against potential enemies. The species presented here are so retiring that other fish can associate with them without any problems.

Care: In tanks 24 inches (60 cm) long or more. Some of the fry may be raised in a community tank if pulverized flakes (in small quantities) are

sprinkled directly into their school with a thin PVC (polyvinyl chloride) tube.
Food: Omnivorous.

Special Tips on Recommended Species of Cichlids

Krib, or purple cichlid (*Pelvicachromis pulcher*); see photo on page 45. Males often almost 4 inches (10 cm) long, females considerably smaller with a reddish spot on their belly). It is best to keep one pair in a 32-inch (80-cm) tank. The krib needs a cave as a territorial center. Even if you keep only one pair, there ought to be two caves, some distance apart, so that the smaller female can retreat in the event of a quarrel with her partner.

Cockatoo or crested dwarf cichlid (*Apistogramma cacatuoides*); see photo on page 45. Males about 2½ to 3 inches (6–8 cm) long, females up to about 2 inches (5 cm). Always keep one male with several females (two in a 24-inch [60-cm] tank, three in a 32-inch [80-cm] tank). Each fish needs its own cave, located at a sufficient distance from the next. These fish are polygamous; that is, a male mates with several females.

Golden, or golden-eyed, dwarf cichlid (*Nannacara anomala*). The males generally are twice as long as the females, which usually have a length of about 2 inches (5 cm). Except at spawning time, it is a peace-loving fish; after spawning, the females are quarrelsome because they are anxious about their brood.

Angelfish, or scalare (*Pterophyllum scalare*); see photos on pages 5 and 43. Up to about 6 inches (15 cm) long and approximately 8 inches (20 cm) high. Needs a tank of at least 32 inches (80 cm) with a minimum height of 20 inches (50 cm). The most important tank decorations are long, tall structures such as the leaves of the black amazon or species of *Anubias barteri*.

Angelfish stay quietly among the plants on lookout.

They live in groups, with the individuals maintaining very short distances from each other. Placid fish, they cannot tolerate lively company. It is best to keep them in a small group of four to six in a 39-inch (1-m) tank that is occupied by other even-tempered fish such as neon tetras, Congo tetras, and black mollies. Do not put them with fin nippers.

<u>Note:</u> The fascinating discus (*Symphysodon discus*), whose brilliant beauty fascinates all aquarists, should not be kept by beginners. It is extremely difficult to take care of.

Ramirez's cichlid, Ram, or butterfly cichlid (*Papiliochromis ramirezi*); see photo on the inside front cover. Up to about 2 inches (5 cm) long. The most peaceable of the cichlids, they pair for life and occupy a small territory. It is especially nice if two pairs are kept in a sufficiently large tank (at least 24 inches [60 cm] long); they frequently come to their territorial boundaries and try to impress each other.

Characins
Order *Characiformes*

Characins are school-forming fish that in their natural habitat travel through the water in mixed or separate schools. They are nimble and often very beautifully colored. These fish suffer without the society of members of the same species. A typical characteristic of this family is the adipose or second dorsal fin—a small fin on the tail stem.

Care: In tanks at least 24 inches (60 cm) long. Dense planting around the tank sides and partial shade provided by floating plants.

Food: Dry food supplemented by freeze-dried or frozen mosquito larvae and vitamins.

Swordfern Microsorium pteropus) is best rooted on wood or stones. Do not set the rhizome in the ground, but bind it to roots or rocks. It will take root on its own.

A dwarf gourami (Colisa lalia) male builds a nest of foam.

Typical reproductive behavior among labyrinth fish. After building a foam nest the male courts a female that is ready to spawn. When she follows him under the nest, he wraps himself around her and turns her onto her back. The female drops several eggs, which the male inseminates and spits into the nest.

Special Tips on Recommended Species of Characins

Neon tetra (*Paracheirodon innesi*); see photo on page 45. About 1 inch (3 cm) long. Because they show to advantage only in a large school, keep at least ten neon tetras. Especially important is a "dark" aquascape in the tank, otherwise these fish appear pale. To darken the bottom covering, plant *Anubias nana* as a ground cover. Roots, dense vegetation around the tank sides, and a partial cover of floating plants.

Require similar care: Cardinal tetra (*Paracheirodon axelrodi*); see photo on page 48; about 1 inch (3 cm) long. Glowlight tetra (*Hemigrammus erythrozonus*); 1½ inches (4 cm) long.

Congo tetra (*Phenacogrammus interruptus*); see photo on page 44. Males about 3 inches (7 cm) long, females 2 to 2½ inches (5–6 cm) long. Keep a small school of six to eight in a tank at least 32 inches (80 cm) long. In light surroundings the bluish iridescent colors of this fish cannot be seen advantage. A peaceable, serene, school-forming fish that dislikes hectic society. Males have elongated dorsal, tail, and anal fins with lustrous white edges. Better not kept in the same tank with tail nippers (although the Congo tetra is fast and can defend itself).

Requires similar care: Long-finned tetra (*Alestes longipinnis*); about 5 inches (13 cm) long; needs a large tank.

Black tetra (*Gymnocorymbus ternezi*). About ¾ to 2⅕ inches (2–5.6 cm) long. A placid fish (livelier when young that travels in schools and inhabits the middle strata of the tank. Its round body shape and black ground color make a nice contrast to slender, colorful fish such as neon tetras.

Requires similar care: *Moenkhausia sanctae filomenae*; see photo on page 44; 2 inches (5 cm) long; inhabits

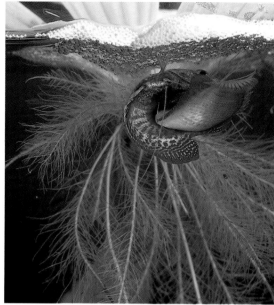

Courtship and spawning...   take place under this nest.

pper portion of tank.

Boehlke's penguin fish (*Thayeria
boehlkei*); 3¼ inches (8.2 cm) long. In
a small school it populates the upper
strata of the tank. As the German
name—"slantwise swimmer"—indicates, this fish lists as it swims and
contrasts nicely with all fish that swim
"straight." Not to be confused with the
so-called "slanters" (*Nannobrycon
eques*), which are somewhat harder to
please with respect to the quality of the
aquarium water.

Rosy tetra (*Hyphessobrycon
rentosi*). About 1½ inches (4 cm) long.
Needs the society of members of its
own species but does not always
travel in a school. The males, which
are prettier, try to impress one another
with their fins extended; they briefly
occupy small courtship territories.

Require similar care: Black phantom
tetra (*Megalamphodus megalopterus*)
and red phantom tetra (*Megalampho-*

dus sweglesi*), each about 1½ inches
(4 cm) long. Emperor tetra (*Nemato-
brycon palmeri*), about 1 inch (3 cm)
long. Black neon tetra (*Hyphessobrycon herbertaxelrodi*), 1½ inches (4 cm)
long. Bleeding heart tetra (*Hyphessobrycon erythrostigma*); see photo on
page 52, 2½ inches (6 cm) long; needs
a tank at least 32 inches (80 cm) long;
goes particularly well with emperor tetra.

Loaches and Sharks
(Bottom-dwelling Carplike Fish)
Order *Cypriniformes*

These species like to stay on the
bottom, where they use their numerous
barbels to search for food. The
loaches have a characteristic feature
that gave them one of their German
names: thorn groundlings. Under each
eye many have a movable spine that
they extend as soon as they are

caught in a net. Be careful: you can injure yourself on the spines.

Care: In tanks at least 24 inches (60 cm) long. Most species are not very demanding in regard to water conditions.

Food: All the usual kinds of foods. You should make sure that bottom dwellers are getting enough food.

Special Tips on Recommended Species of Loaches

Red-tailed shark (*Labeo bicolor*); see photo on page 28. About 6 inches (15 cm) long. Needs tanks 32 to 39 inches (80 cm to 1 m) long. In smaller tanks keep only a single fish, because these sharks occupy territories and defend them against members of their own species. They may get rough with other tankmates as well. Put them together only with fast, small fish or larger, more easygoing ones. If you want to keep several of them in larger tanks, never have two; three or more will fare better. Each fish needs its own hiding place.

<u>Requires similar care:</u> *Labeo frenatus*. About 5½ inches (14 cm) long, but less aggressive, hence several can be kept in a 39-inch (1-m) tank.

Clown loach (*Botia macracantha*); see photo on page 29: About 3½ to 6⅓ inches (9–16 cm) long; in its natural habitat up to about 12 inches (30 cm) long. An extremely beautiful species, which develops fully only in large tanks. You may keep several young clown loaches, but only a single mature one. This fish, with its somewhat trunklike elongated mouth, can even pull snails out of their shells and eat them.

<u>Requires similar care:</u> Dwarf loach (*Botia sidthimunchi*). Up to 2½ inches (6 cm) long. A lively, school-forming fish. Keep no fewer than five in your tank.

[*Echinodorus osiris, a type of water plantain, is one of the classic aquarium plants. Its reddish leaves enliven the aquascape.*

Rainbow Fish
Family *Melanotaeniidae*

This family of fish has grown in popularity in recent years because many new species that are easy to care for are being introduced and bred. Their colors glow most intensely in the morning hours, when courtship and spawning occur. The colors appear especially lovely when a little sunlight shines on them from the side.

Care: In tanks between 32 and 39 inches (80–100 cm) long. Dense vegetation, but a great deal of open swimming space. Sensitive to a pH below 7.

Food: All the usual kinds of foods.

Special Tips on Recommended Species of Rainbow Fish

Boeseman's rainbow fish (*Melanotaenia boesemani*); see photo on page 45: Males up to 4 inches (10 cm) long, females, up to slightly over 3 inches (8 cm). A lively, school-forming fish (keep five to seven of them) that is most active in the morning. It likes to spawn on Java moss. A dark background in your tank will emphasize the golden orange color.

<u>Require similar care:</u> Most other *Melanotaenia* species. The jewel rainbow fish (*Melanotaenia trifasciatus*), 4¾ inches (12 cm) long, is well known.

Salmon pink rainbow fish (*Glossolepis incisus*); see photo on page 44. A school-forming fish up to 6 inches (15 cm) long. Because it needs a great deal of swimming space, set plants only along the rear wall and sides. Cushions of Java moss are an ideal spawning site for these rainbow fish as well. In a group of salmon pink rainbow fish, only the strongest male has a splendid pinkish orange color, while the other males remain a darker, muddier pink. If you remove the dominant male from the tank, the next strongest one will change his color.

Food Selection and Feeding

What Foods to Give

Once it was a point of honor for aquarists to feed their fish with foods that they themselves had caught outdoors. On walks through the countryside, the landing net was always brought along to fish insect larvae, water fleas, and worms from the nearest marshy pool or creek. That is hardly possible today. First, bodies of water are growing increasingly scarce, and those still in existence are often badly polluted. The danger of bringing pathogenic organisms into the aquarium by this feeding method is simply too great. Second, one can easily run afoul of the wildlife conservation laws, because many animals and their larvae (amphibians, for example) are protected by law, and in catching water fleas one can all too easily get a couple of tadpoles in the net. Using the foods offered in pet stores, you can readily put together varied menus for your pets.

Dry Food

Dry food is available in the form of flakes, tablets, or granulated pellets. It contains all the vital nutrients in sufficient quantity, as well as ample roughage (to stimulate bowel function). Dry food represents your fishes' "meat and potatoes."

Flaked food comes in various sizes. Fry and small species get the small flakes, large fish eat the big ones, and all fish will accept the medium-size flakes. In selecting flaked food keep in mind the special requirements of your pets. Species that prefer a vegetarian diet need flakes with a large percentage of "green stuff" (to determine the composition, see the package).

Food tablets are used for fish that feed on the bottom; simply let them drop to the bottom of the tank. There are also tablets that can be stuck to the aquarium pane, where they are readily available to all the fish.

Granulated pellets, so-called "crumb food" (of very high nutritive

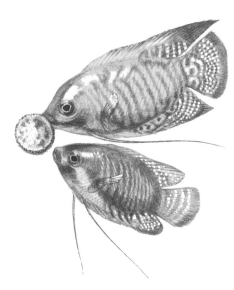

Two dwarf gouramis nibble at a food tablet that is stuck to the aquarium pane.

They gleam like gold: half-striped barbs (Puntius semifasciolatus).

value), usually are not accepted right away by most fish. After some time, however, they become accustomed to the pellets. It is best to give your pets pellets and flakes alternately.

Frozen Food

Frozen food, a good substitute for live food, consists of deep-frozen food animals such as mosquito larvae and water fleas. Any germs present are killed by the freezing process. This is a valuable supplement to dry food. Frozen food has to be kept in the freezer. Be sure not to take out more than you plan to use at one feeding.

Freeze-dried Food

Freeze-dried food consists of food animals that are frozen in a special process, at the end of which they are ried. Freeze-dried food is suitable as supplementary food.

Vitamin Concentrates

These are a very important addition to your pets' diet. A few drops given regularly (sprinkled over frozen food) will meet the fish's requirements.

What Foods Not to Give

• Tubifex (tube-dwelling worms) live in the mud of heavily polluted bodies of water and can cause disease.
• Kitchen leftovers do not belong in the aquarium, where they rapidly can impair the water quality.
• As a beginner do not try to feed your fish lettuce or spinach leaves. Instead provide herbivorous fish with vegetarian food from the pet store.
• Live food is sold in many pet stores or advertised in aquarium magazines. You also can raise it yourself, although the danger that you—as a novice—will make mistakes and bring germs into the aquarium is quite great. Therefore, I recommend that you wait until you are more experienced.

How to Feed

Flakes, pellets, and freeze-dried foods should be sprinkled through the feeding hole in the tank cover.

Tablets should be pressed onto the glass pane—if possible, the front pane—so that you will know how much has been eaten. Alternatively, drop them into the water.

Frozen food is sold in sheets, divided into cubes of 0.061 cubic inches (1 cubic cm). For smaller fish that run no risk of swallowing a cube whole, put the unthawed cubes in the water. They will float on the surface, thaw slowly, and appear to be in motion. They will be eaten by fish that otherwise react only to some movement of their prey. For large fish thaw the food in a dish before using it. Otherwise the fish

A moss green Sumatra barb (Puntius tetrazona).

A harlequin rasbora (Rasbora heteromorpha).

would swallow the cubes while still frozen, and diseases of their digestive organs would result.

How Much to Feed

In my experience people who are still learning about fish care give their pets far too much food. It is not so easy to ignore the sight of a school of fish that usually rush at once to the front pane upon seeing their caretaker and appear to beg hungrily for food. I can only urge you strongly that it is

41

better to feed too little rather than too much. Animals that constantly gorge themselves become highly susceptible to disease.

Basic rules for the correct amount are as follows:

• Offer only as much food as your fish will eat in a very short time. Flakes should sink no deeper than one-third of the height of the tank (provide tablets for bottomfeeders). In this way there will be no leftover food to impair the water quality.

• Feed several small portions, one after another.

• If you are home during the day, spread out the portions over the course of the day. If you can feed your pets only in the morning and evening, be sure you take time to do so slowly and in portions.

My suggestion: If your hand should slip while feeding your pets, siphon off the food as you would the decayed matter when you change the water (see page 50). Wash the filter in the next few days to prevent adulteration with food remnants.

Feeding during Vacation

A well-tended aquarium can be left to itself for two or three weeks. You need have no qualms about going on vacation provided that you have made arrangements for feeding the fish. Fish can get by without food for an occasional weekend, but for a longer absence I advise you to install an automatic food dispenser. These dispensers are available in various models.

Important: Install the dispenser at least two weeks before your vacation begins so that the fish can get used to it and you can learn to estimate the correct portions. If necessary lengthen the intervals between feedings so that the fish will finish what is offered.

Mouth shapes provide information about the way fish eat:
a) A mouth opening that is directed upward is used to take food from the water surface.
b) Fish with a mouth directed forward find their food in open water.
c) All groundfish, which search for food on the bottom, have a mouth opening that points downward.

Important Feeding Rules at a Glance

1. Feed your fish only when you have time to see whether all of them are eating. Refusal to eat is a sure indication of illness.

2. Feed only as much as is eaten at one time. The food should not sink to the bottom. One exception: tablets provided for bottom feeders must sink to the bottom.

3. Offer a variety of foods.

4. First use flakes as a basic food, then offer frozen or freeze-dried food as a treat.

5. Never feed if you have just turned on the light. Your fish won't be fully alert until 30 minutes later.

6. Never feed if you have just performed some aquarium maintenance procedure (after changing the water, cleaning the panes, and the like).

7. Don't crumble the flakes; the fish need to "work" for their food.

8. If several members of your family share in the care of the aquarium, choose one person to handle the feeding. It will be clear whose responsibility it is.

9. Never switch the filter off when you feed the fish. Otherwise the food will be siphoned off. If flakes do get into the filter, the portion was too large. (If this happens, clean the filter.)

10. For longer absences install an automated food dispenser (see Feeding during Vacation, *left*). Never try to create a "stock" of food. The food will spoil the water, and the catastrophe will have been preprogrammed.

Aquarium Care Made Easy

The Water Habitat

What air is for humans, water is for fish. Just as we feel at ease in clean, good air, our wards need water that is good and clean. This is achieved through regular upkeep. To understand the maintenance procedures involved, you need to know what actually constitutes good water for fish. The decisive factors are the acidity of the water (pH), the hardness of the water, the nitrite-nitrate content, and the gases released in water from air: oxygen and carbon dioxide.

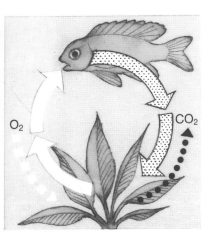

Exchange of oxygen (O_2) and carbon dioxide (CO_2) between fish and plant.

Water Acidity

The acidity of the water is expressed in pH units. Neutral water has a pH of 7. Values from 0 to 6.9 are indicative of acid water, while values from 7.1 to 14 lie within the alkaline range. Most tropical aquarium fish prefer a range between 6.5 and 7.5. Naturally some fishes are exceptions, but the majority of those listed in this book feel comfortable in this range.

Measuring the pH: Pet stores carry test kits with reagents that can quickly tell you the pH.

Changing the pH: Tap water usually has pH values slightly above 7. As a rule, then, you can use tap water in setting up your aquarium. However, you should measure the pH after a few days have passed. If it is in the specified range you can put the fish in the tank. If necessary the pH can be lowered. The simplest method is to add pH-reducing agents and—somewhat harder to deal with—peat extracts. In so doing it is important to check the pH value both during the procedure and one or two days after its completion.

Important: The pH should be checked at regular intervals as part of routine maintenance.

Water Hardness

The total hardness is measured in degrees of hardness (dH), as follows:
2–8 dH = soft
9–16 dH = medium hard
17–30 dH = hard

Carbon dioxide is constantly exchanged between fish and plants. By day the fish inhales oxygen (O_2) and exhales carbon dioxide (CO_2). The plant takes in carbon dioxide and produces oxygen. At night the fish and plants breathe oxygen and give off carbon dioxide.

Fascinating aquarium fish that make good tankmates: The krib and cockatoo dwarf cichlids are cichlids; the Boeseman's rainbow fish and salmon pink rainbow fish are rainbow fish; *Moenkhausia sanctae filomenae*, the neon tetra, and the Congo tetra are characins; and the bronze catfish and brittle-mouth catfish are catfish.

Moenkhausia sanctae filomenae.

Congo tetra.

Salmon pink rainbow fish.

Brittle-mouth catfish (Ancistrus spec.).

Boeseman's rainbow fish.

Krib (Pelvicachromis pulcher).

Cockatoo dwarf cichlid.

Neon tetras (Paracheirodon innesi).

Bronze catfish (Corydoras aeneus).

F or the upkeep of your aquarium follow the rule "in moderation, but with regularity." This way you will not disturb your pets too often, and you will create the best possible habitat for them with little effort. Among the most crucial procedures is maintenance of the water, filter, and plants.

You can find out how hard your tap water is by contacting the local water department. If the degree of hardness of your water falls in the range of soft to medium hard, most fish will be comfortable in it. If the water is harder, you will have to soften it.

Softening the water: The easiest method for the beginner is to soften the water by using "Aqua top" or similar products that are available in pet stores. They consist of so-called flood bags that you hang in the water like tea bags. The graphic instructions for their use will tell you how and for what period of time to employ them. Beyond that you need only know that the so-called carbonate hardness is a component of total hardness. Carbonate hardness, which plays an important role in water hardness, can be measured with the use of reagents.

Note: I do not recommend that beginners try the peat filtration method used by experienced aquarists and the softening equipment available in pet stores.

Waste Products in the Aquarium

Even in well-maintained aquariums a great deal of debris is constantly produced. It consists of organic waste products that result from the elimination of the fish, superfluous food, and decaying animal and plant parts. These waste products continually undergo a process of transformation brought about by the bacteria present in the soil, in the filter, and in the water. In this process nitrite—poisonous to fish—is created, then transformed into less dangerous nitrate. Major assistance in this process, in which oxygen is consumed, is provided by the plants. This means that there are usually no problems with the nitrite-nitrate content—that is, as long as enough oxygen is present; your tank contains a good, diverse selection of plants; and the filter works perfectly.

Dangers for the fish arise only if they live in a tank where the plants do not thrive or have enough diversity, or where the water is badly polluted. In such tanks the nitrite-nitrate content is "thrown out of joint." At first the well-being of the fish will not be affected but when the oxygen is depleted or when maintenance procedures (such as changing the water or cleaning the filter) are performed, the fish will exhibit symptoms of poisoning: they will come to the water surface and gasp for air, and they will refuse to eat. Anyone who has let things get to this stage will have to take immediate measures. For small tanks it is best to empty the entire tank and set it up again from scratch. In a 53-gallon (200-L) tank you can try to save whatever can be saved.

Emergency Program for Badly Neglected Aquariums

The following measures must be performed for two or three weeks:
- Add oxygen continually.
- Carefully loosen the bottom soil with your fingers so that any sewage gas present can escape. Do not churn up the bottom material.
- Change one-third of the water at once and every subsequent week for three weeks.
- Clean the filter immediately and again two weeks later.
- Do not feed the fish for the first three days.
- Add Biocoryn H3 to the water as the instructions direct.
- After three weeks switch to the normal routine for aquarium upkeep.
- Generally this emergency program will help. Some fish and plants, however, may not survive the procedure.

My suggestion: By taking good care of the water, filter, and plants, you can avoid all the problems that organic waste products cause.

Algae and Measures to Combat Them

Type of algae	Countermeasures
Beard algae: brownish-black, very tenacious, frequently occur on swordfern.	Cut off badly affected leaves. Introduce algae eaters such as half-striped, ruby, or Sumatra barbs.
Brush algae: brownish-black, free-floating, sometimes on rocks or plants.	Siphon off gravel and freely suspended algae; throw the gravel away. Introduce algae eaters such as flying foxes, half-striped and ruby barbs, black mollies, guppies, and platies.
Gravel algae (diatoms): blackish-green spots on leaf blades, common in *Anubias* and *Echinodorus* species, usually on old leaves.	Do not remove the affected leaves. Introduce algae eaters such as bristle-mouth catfish or other armored catfish.
Blue-green algae: bluish-black to dark green, can be rubbed off easily, smell of ammonia.	Add iron-rich fertilizer. Temperature not above 75° F (24° C). Introduce algae eaters such as Japanese bitterling.
Brown algae: slightly brownish coating on leaves, rocks, and panes	Introduce algae eaters such as sucker-mouth catfish and blue bristle-mouth catfish.
Thread algae (confer va): spin a cottony web first around stems, then everything else	Add iron-rich fertilizer. Introduce algae eaters such as flying foxes, black mollies, or sailfin mollies. Plant rapidly growing plants such as waterweed.
Volvox (green) algae: pea green water	Don't change the water. Use a diatom filter or ultraviolet light (ask your pet store dealer), along with an oxidizer.
Slimy, light green film everywhere in aquarium.	Change water. Plant rapidly growing plants such as waterweed and water wisteria.
Furry, brownish-black film on leaf lades that cannot be rubbed off.	Introduce algae eaters such as flying fox, blue bristle-mouth catfish, armored catfish, guppy, black molly.

Important: When you introduce algae eaters into the aquarium, do not put food in the tank for one week.

Beard algae develop long, threadlike growths that are brownish-black in color.

Brush algae are also brownish-black. They are freely suspended in the water or grow on plants and rocks.

Neon tetras, which are very colorful against the dark bottom covering, nibble at a food tablet.

Oxygen and Carbon Dioxide

Oxygen and carbon dioxide, both gases, play an important role in the life of the plants and animals in an aquarium.

Oxygen is required by both animals and plants. A good growth of vegetation and a water surface kept in motion by the filter guarantee the most natural supply of oxygen. If an additional supply of oxygen is needed, use airstones and air diffusers. The quickest and best method is to use a so-called oxidizer (follow the directions exactly).

When there is insufficient oxygen the fish gasp for breath and swim right under the water surface. If this happens, add oxygen immediately. If their behavior does not improve, check to see whether the water has been contaminated by adverse conditions, and take appropriate measures (see table, pages 58–59).

Carbon dioxide (CO_2) is produced

during the respiration of fish and also by the bacteria in the filter and in the tank bottom. It is an important plant nutrient. Because the plants in the aquarium consume large quantities of CO_2, an additional supply must be kept on hand. For this purpose use the simple CO_2 systems recommended for beginners on page 8.

Filter Maintenance

The coarser filter materials, like foam and the coarse biosubstrate, are simply mechanical filtering media. Over time bacteria settle on them and decompose the debris caught there. In this process plant nutrients—including carbon dioxide—are liberated, and thus the filter material becomes a biological filter. This process works only if the filter is maintained satisfactorily.

Maintenance of the inside filter: Every two to four weeks (depending on the fish population) wash out the foam material with lukewarm water (without adding detergents), press out the water, and reuse the filter. When the foam loses its shape, replace it with a new cartridge.

Maintenance of the outside filter: Wash the substrate with lukewarm water every three or four months, rinsing it until the water is clear. Follow the directions for use. When changing the filter material, reuse about one third of the old substrate.

Important: Never wash filter materials in water that is more than lukewarm (about 86° F [30° C]). Never boil it or disinfect it; that would destroy the filter bacteria.

Timetable for Periodic Maintenance Procedures

Daily: Check the temperature and inspect the equipment. Add CO_2. Check the state of your pets' health (see page 55).

Weekly: Change one-third of the water and siphon off loose debris and leaves (see page 50). Add one tablet of fertilizer for every 13 gallons (50 L) of water. Add a water conditioner that will not harm the mucous membranes of the fish. Measure and regulate the water quality. Clean the panes (see page 50).

Monthly: Trim the plants (see page 51). Clean the filter.

Every six months: Replace the hoses (they become hard and are no longer reliable). Replace the fluorescent tube (if you have two, replace one every three months).

When necessary: Siphon off food remnants. Remove dead plant leaves and dead fish, and pick up snails.

Important: In order to disturb the fish as little as possible, don't perform more than one maintenance task per day.

How-To
Aquarium Maintenance

Taking care of an aquarium is not a complicated business—at least, as long as you do it regularly. The tasks called for are described below. Before beginning your cleaning chores, pull all the plugs, without fail.

Changing the Water
Illustration 1

I recommend that you replace one-third of the water once a week. (Not more, otherwise the water quality will change too drastically.) Theoretically you could simply scoop out the water, but it is faster with a hose and a bucket.

Here's how to do it: Take a hose about 5 feet (1.5 m) long, with a diameter of 12 to 16 millimeters, and fill it with water at the tap or in a sink full of water (same temperature as the aquarium water). Holding the hose ends closed with your thumbs, put one end into the aquarium, which should be at a higher level, and the other into the bucket, placed at a lower level. This dif-ference in height is important; without it, the water will not drain. First

open the end you have placed in the aquarium, then the one in the bucket, and the water will start to flow at once. The suction will be powerful enough to siphon off food remnants, debris, and algae along with the water. While moving the hose around the aquarium with one hand, keep the other on the hose in the bucket. Then you can stop the flow quickly if a fish gets too near the mouth of the hose and is siphoned off. If this does happen, pour the water in the bucket through a net and replace the fish in the tank.

Siphoning off Debris
Illustration 2

Over time you will observe that a brown layer of debris forms on the aquarium bottom, especially in the corners. This debris is a mixture of dead parts of plants and fish excrement. It must be removed from time to time, because too much oxygen is consumed when it is broken down by bacteria. You can siphon it off when you change the water or use a so-called debris siphon, moving it carefully back and forth over the gravel. Debris and water will go into the pail, while the heavier gravel falls back to the bottom. Never press down too hard on the gravel, or you will destroy the fine structure of the plants' root network.

Cleaning the Panes

Get in the habit of cleaning the aquarium panes, inside and outside, once a week. For cleaning the outside it is enough simply to wipe off the panes with a damp cloth. A practical solution for cleaning the inside panes

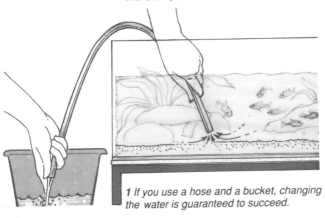

1 If you use a hose and a bucket, changing the water is guaranteed to succeed.

is the so-called algae magnet. If you use pane scrapers that have a razor blade, be careful not to cut into the silicon layer that coats the aquarium.

Important: Do not use detergents to clean the panes.

Plant Cultivation

If the plants in the aquarium are to remain biologically efficient, produce oxygen, absorb waste products, and develop their other water-cleansing properties, they need the best possible care.

Fertilizing

For healthy growth, the plants need additional nutrients. Use fertilizers made for aquarium plants, iron-rich fertilizer, and CO_2.

Rules for fertilizing:
- In using fertilizers, follow the dosage instructions on the package exactly.
- Fertilize when you first set up the tank and again after every change of water.
- Liquid fertilizers can be used in aquariums even if there is no long-term fertilizer in the bottom material.
- Keep CO_2 on hand (page 8).

Cutting and Thinning Out

If the vegetation grows too luxuriant, trim the plants or thin them out at regular intervals. From time to time fish out the floating plants and remove by hand any large dead parts that cannot be siphoned off when the water is changed.

Cutting back stem plants:
Illustrations 3 to 5

There are many rapidly growing species of stem plants that must be kept in check. If you notice that a plant is beginning to stretch along the surface of the water, shorten it. Using scissors or a sharp knife, cut off two-thirds of the plant (see illustration 3). After only two weeks, you will be able to see two new shoots (see illustration 4). The plant will grow bushier. This process may be repeated.

If you cut off too little, the plant will put out runners directly below the water surface. These will cast a large shadow, and the leaves lower down will be deprived of light. Then the plant will shed the lower leaves and grow increasingly leafless and ugly. Even incorrectly trimmed plants, however, can be brought back "into shape." Simply bend the stem to the bottom and weight it with a rock (see illustration 5). As soon as the stem has struck root, separate it from the stool, or mother plant. Now it can grow just as bushy.

2 Carefully move the debris siphon over the gravel.

3 The plant is too long and must be trimmed by two thirds.

4 The result of proper trimming. The plant puts forth new shoots.

5 If necessary, weight long shoots to keep them on the bottom.

Algae are found in every aquarium. They are just as much a part of it as fish, plants, and bacteria. An increase in algal growth, however, is an indication that something is amiss in the aquarium. In this case, determine the causes and take appropriate measures.

Angelfish and bleeding heart tetras.

Snails in the Aquarium

Snails are the "garbage disposal service" of the aquarium: they eradicate food remnants, dying plant matter, algae, and dead fish. You probably will be surprised to discover snails in your aquarium without your having bought any. They are carried in by the plants, which usually have some snail spawn on them.

If snails become rampant, overfeeding usually is the cause. The better the food situation, the more rapidly the animals multiply. If this is the case, you easily can set up a kind of "snail trap." First feed the fish, then put one or two food tablets on a flat stone. After some time more and more snails will appear there. You only need to pick them up and—the best solution—put them in the compost heap.

The Aquarium during Vacation

If you don't have someone who can be relied on to take care of your aquarium during your absence, make a few preparations:
• A few weeks before your vacation starts do not introduce any more new fish to the tank. Otherwise you will have no control over problems that may occur (diseases that have been carried in or territorial fighting).
• Two weeks in advance, install an automatic food dispenser and use it exclusively.
• Three days before departure wash out the inside filter. (Outside filters can go four months without being cleaned.)
• Two days in advance change one-third of the water, being sure to siphon off the debris, and add a water conditioner.
• The day before inspect all the equipment to see whether it is working.

Algae in the Aquarium

There is no aquarium without algae. Algae are just as much a part of it as the plants, fish, and bacteria. In a well-maintained aquarium algae eaters keep a tight rein on the algae. Algae become a problem if they grow rampant, that is, become clearly visible. An increase in algal growth serves as an alarm signal; it alerts you to the fact that something is amiss in the aquarium. Take appropriate measures. Trying to control algae, however, does not mean that you reach for suitable chemicals, but that you first ascertain the causes and correct the situation. If there are not too many things wrong at once, the problem usually will solve itself as soon as you have remedied matters. Otherwise you will have to make a concerted effort to combat the algae (see table, page 47).

How to discover the causes of increased algal growth: To trace these causes, you will have to check out the entire aquarium:
• Is the filter clean?
• Is the period of daylight correct? Do the fluorescent tubes need to be replaced?
• Have you changed the water periodically?
• Is the temperature correct?
• Are the carbon dioxide (CO_2) and oxygen contents correct?
• Is the nitrite-nitrate content right?
• Is the pH correct?
• Is the water hardness right?
• Are there enough algae eaters in the aquarium?
If you have answered any questions with "no," remedy the situation, then wait and see.

Snails are the aquarium's garbage disposal service. These kinds are common:
a) Red ramshorn snail.
b) Malayan snail.
c) South American mystery snail.

Emergency Aid for Breakdowns in the Aquarium

Indication	Cause	Remedy
Inside filter makes noises audible 39 inches (1 cm) away.	1. Dirty filter. 2. Axle worn out, for example, by fine sand.	1. Replace filter cartridge. 2. Replace driving magnet and axle.
Outside filter knocks, power drops.	Axle worn out (by fine sand or substrate that has not been washed in advance).	Replace driving magnet, axle, and axle bearing.
Outside filter hisses suddenly.	1. Compacted filter material is forming sewage gases that are expelled in gusts. 2. Old hoses are drawing air, or a gasket is not tight.	1. Wash filter material or replace part of it. 2. Install new hoses or new gasket.
Water is brownish-green, fish swim at the surface.	Filter has stopped or is completely fouled.	Change ⅓ of water; increase oxygen content. Wash filter material; connect filter, and give no food for 3 days.
Water is cloudy and whitish, clear in the morning but "white cloud" present in evening under fluorescent light, fish at water surface.	Bacterial clouding; bacteria sink to bottom at night and seek the light during the day.	Siphon off debris and food remnants, clean filter, increase oxygen content, kill bacteria (agent available in pet stores), give no food for 3 days.
Water is clear, but all fish are at water surface.	Temperature too high (chiefly in summer).	Don't change water; it would put the fish in shock. Adjust heater, increase oxygen content, check filter; give no food for 3 days, until the fish breathe normally.
Aquarium leaks.	——	Have it professionally repaired.
Dampness around aquarium, panes undamaged.	1. Water level lowered by evaporation; filter sprays water as a result. 2. Filter hoses not watertight. 3. Diffuser improperly attached. 4. Filter gasket defective.	1. Add water and keep an eye on tank. 2. Replace hoses. 3. Attach diffuser properly. 4. Replace gasket.
Temperature drops.	Heater defective.	Buy a new heater; give no food for 2 days.
Water clouded with flakes of food.	Overfeeding.	Clean filter. Siphon off flakes while you replace 9/10 of the water (add conditioning agent); increase oxygen content, give no food for 5 to 6 days, then clean filter.
Air bubbles rise from bottom material.	Sewage gases.	Loosen bottom soil with fingers; change ⅓ of water; be more careful when feeding tablets to fish.
White "threads" on bottom.	Putrefactive fungi at feeding site.	Siphon off while water is changed; carefully loosen bottom soil with fingers.
Foam on water surface.	1. Decaying food remnants. 2. Foam nest (see photo, page 36).	1. Change water, clean filter. 2. Leave alone.
White "fuzz" in water.	Slime particles after filter has been cleaned.	Not necessary.

Important: Whenever working with electrical appliances, pull the plug!

Diseases and Their Treatment

Prevention Is Better Than a Cure

Pathogenic organisms—parasites, bacteria, and viruses—are present in every aquarium. They may be brought in by new fish and plants, for example. It depends on the resistance of your fish, however, whether diseases actually break out. Poor living conditions weaken your pets' powers of resistance. For this reason direct your attention to keeping the fish and the entire aquarium healthy. If you follow a few basic rules, an outbreak of disease usually can be prevented or at least made less likely.

How to Recognize Diseases

You can tell that a fish does not feel well by its appearance and its behavior. Use feeding time to observe the fish and give your aquarium a searching glance at intervals each day. The sooner you notice changes, the faster and more effectively you can intervene.

Changes in behavioral patterns may occur: refusal to eat; accelerated gill activity, fish gasping for air just below the water surface, hectic darting around; leaping; fish that scarcely move at all, twitching of fins, rubbing, pressing fins close to the body, bobbing up and down, turning around, swaying, wobbling.

External symptoms of disease: See illustration below.

Note: Common diseases of fish are listed in the table on pages 58 and 59.

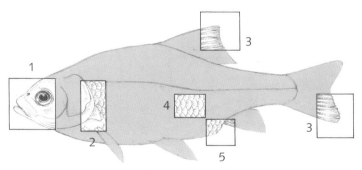

Symptoms of disease in various areas of the body:
1. *Head area: pitted with holes; dull eyes; bulging eyes; white film near mouth.*
2. *Gills: reddened (occurs naturally in many fish, of course); faded; worms protruding; gill covers stretched apart; white spots.*
3. *Fins: frayed or shortened; cottony film; white spots.*
4. *Scales and skin: protruding scales; little blisters; tumors; discolorations; fading; heavy mucus secretion; spots ranging from white to yellowish; red, open places.*
5. *Anal area: swollen; worms protruding; long, stringy, or mucous excrement.*

A dwarf gourami (Colisa lalia) that has strayed into the bottom portion of the aquarium.

What to Do in Case of Illness

Because diseases often spread throughout the aquarium, it is important to take remedial measures at once. The following tips should be helpful:
• Only a few veterinarians are experienced in treating diseases of fish, and they generally are not available immediately. Many pet store dealers, however, can provide quick, reliable help.
• Make a note of all changes in behavior and symptoms of illness so that you can give the pet store dealer as detailed a clinical picture as possible.
• Don't reach indiscriminately for some medicine. So-called broad-band treatment with a single medicine that allegedly is good for everything is of little use. For successful treatment you need a medicine precisely suited to the specific disease. Pet store dealers will guide you in selecting one.
• In medicating your pets follow the prescribed dosages exactly. To give the proper dose you obviously need to know how much water is in your tank.

Two blue snakeskin gouramis (Trichogaster trichopterus).

Important: Never use medications and water conditioning agents simultaneously, or the effect of the medications will be largely neutralized.
• Make sure the oxygen content is high (see page 48).
• Clean the filter (don't use charcoal filtration while administering medications simultaneously).
• Try to determine the causes and, if possible, take remedial measures.

Note: As a rule the entire aquarium population has to be treated. Usually little is gained by placing sick fish in a quarantine tank, because apparently healthy fish may already be carrying the pathogens.

Supportive Measures
A kind of "sauna method" used in combination with other measures often works real miracles. When the temperature is raised, the disease-causing organisms multiply. A complete outbreak of the disease results, and the medication is able to reach all the organisms before they become encysted again.

White spot disease, or Ichthyophthirius multifiliis.

Ascites, or abdominal bloating.

Fungal infection.

Fin rot.

The Most Common Diseases of Fish and

Symptom	Diagnosis
White spots on fins and body; loss of appetite, swaying, and twitching of fins.	White spot disease (drawing, *left*).
Fish grows increasingly fat and threatens to "burst"; scales protrude.	Ascites (drawing, *le*
Cottony, moldlike patches.	Injury to mucus membrane resultin in fungal infection (drawing, *left*).
Colors fade; fish gasp for breath at water surface; erratic swimming movements such as swaying, turning about, and bumping into things.	Chemical poisonin
Colors fade slowly; fish become listless and swim at a slant or on their side; skin in eye area becomes dull, eyes begin to bulge; breathing accelerates.	Slow poisoning du unfavorable water conditions.
Sudden appearance of spots on skin, which looks as though peppered with fine powder, easily visible from the front. Spots are more yellowish than white.	Velvet disease.
Loss of appetite; discoloration; whitish, mucous excrement; holes in the head.	Hole disease.
Breathing exceedingly rapid, head rubbed against objects, mouth bulges in and out jerkily; colorless, threadlike worms protrude from gills.	Parasitic gill worms
Bulging eyes.	Popeye, or exophthalmia.
Fins fray and degenerate, discoloration.	Fin rot (drawing, *le*
Colors fade, starting at the midsection of the body. The area extends like a belt as the disease progresses.	Neon tetra disease

uses	Treatment
rasite (*Ichthyophthirius multifiliis*).	Appropriate medications and supportive measures (page 60).
cterial infection or metabolic disturbance due to ong food or too much food.	Difficult. If possible separate the affected fish. Stimulate metabolism with salt (0.04 ounces/quart) (1 gram/liter), increase oxygen content and temperature. Give medications.
uries to mucus membrane resulting in its degen- ation.	Appropriate medications. As a supportive measure, increase oxygen content. Change ⅓ of water, adding no conditioning agent. Give additional vitamins. After treatment, clean filter.
tergents in aquarium bucket; overfertilization; hair ay or pesticide used near aquarium; water from mineralization facilities for pipe decalcification.	Almost total water change (⅘). Use a water conditioning agent that will protect the mucus membranes. No feeding. Test filter to see if enough water is passing through. Take remedial measures. Watch fish carefully; lowered resistance makes them susceptible to other diseases.
favorable water conditions after large-scale aning of aquarium. You have done too much at e time. Wrong water, such as rain water; nitrate- rite content too high; pH too high; sewage gases bottom; inappropriate decorative materials; im- per transfer of fish; mucus membrane injured.	Change ⅓ of water. Add Biocoryn H3. Add oxygen. Take remedial measures.
rasite (*Oodinium pillularis*).	Treat with appropriate medications and take supportive measures (page 60).
estation of *Hexamita*, protozoan carried into tank.	Increase oxygen content. Slowly raise temperature to 91° F (33° C) if all the fish can tolerate it. Otherwise treat with appropriate medications.
l parasites carried in.	Raise oxygen content. Treat with appropriate medications.
or water quality, with metabolic disturbances as a sult.	Raise oxygen content. Clean filter, change ⅓ of water every 3 days until water conditions are normal; add conditioning agent. No food for 2 to 3 days.
ury during transport; wasting parasite; lack of ygen.	Raise oxygen content. Change ⅓ of water, clean filter. Appropriate medications.
rasite (*Plistophora*).	Very difficult. Use appropriate medications. Success is rare. Vitamin supplements as a supportive measure.

Here's how to do it:

1. Change one-third of the water, but do not add a water conditioning agent; the substances it contains will combine with the medications and render them ineffective.

2. Raise the temperature a total of about 7° F (4° C) over two days, or about 3.5° F (2° C) each day. The maximum temperature possible in the average aquarium is just under 90° F (32° C).

3. Administer the medication in the specified dosage. Too low a dose results in the formation of resistant strains of the organisms.

4. Give no food for three or four days.

5. As a rule the external symptoms of a disease will have disappeared after one week. Then lower the temperature again, feed as usual, and give additional vitamins. Otherwise leave the aquarium alone.

6. After one more week change one-third of the water and add a conditioning agent.

7. Check the filter to see whether enough water is passing through.

What to Do after Giving Medication

After treating your pets with medications, it may be necessary (for example, if the water is discolored) to filter the water through charcoal. Filter charcoal is a chemical filtering material that alters the composition of the aquarium water. Put the dry filter charcoal into a filter bag and cover it with filter wadding, which will retain the coal dust. The effectiveness of the charcoal will be exhausted after about one week, after which it should be thrown away. Do not reuse it!

Important: Use charcoal filtration only for the purpose mentioned, because vitally important substances such as water conditioners and nutrients are also removed from the water during this process.

Most Important Rules for a Healthy Aquarium

1. A well-functioning filter is essential for keeping the water clean.

2. The diversity of the plants and the proper growth of the vegetation are important. In selecting plants keep this in mind, then cultivate them properly. (see Plant Cultivation, page 51).

3. Make sure there is enough oxygen in the water (see page 48).

4. Don't put too many fish in your tank, and place together only those species that get along with each other and require the same living conditions.

5. Buy only healthy fish (see How to Recognize Diseases, page 55).

6. Change the water regularly, adding a water conditioning agent that will protect the mucus membranes.

7. Avoid sudden drops in temperature when the water is changed.

8. Keep an eye on the pH and other water conditions.

9. Feed the fish regularly, using a varied selection of foods, and—above all—feed them properly (see pages 39-42).

10. Regularly use vitamin preparations appropriate for fish (available in pet stores).

11. Never perform more than one maintenance procedure in the same day.

12. Remove dead animals immediately.

Index

Addresses and Suggestions for Furthe Reading

Books

Braemer, Helga and Ines
    Scheurmann: *Tropical Fish*
    (Barron's, 1983).

Hansen, J.: *Making Your Own
    Aquarium* (Bell and Hyman,
    1979).

Hawkins, A.D. (Editor): *Aquarium
    Systems* (Academic Press,
    1981).

Kahl, Burkard: *Aquarium Fish Mini
    Fact Finder* (Barron's, 1990).

Ramshorst, J. D. van (Editor): *The
    Complete Aquarium Encyclo-
    pedia* (Phaidon, 1978).

Scheurmann, Ines: *Aquarium Fish
    Breeding* (Barron's, 1990).

————: *The New Aquarium
    Handbook* (Barron's, 1986).

————: *Water Plants in the
    Aquarium* (Barron's, 1987)

Sterba, G.: *The Aquarists' Ency
    pedia* (Blandford, 1983).

Ward, Brian: *Aquarium Fish Sur
    Manual* (Barron's, 1985).

Magazines

Aquarium Fish Magazine
P.O. Box 6050
Mission Viejo, CA 92690

Freshwater and Marine Aquariu
144 West Sierra Madre Bouleva
Sierra Madre, CA 91024

Practical Fishkeeping Magazine
RR1, Box 200D
Jonesburg, MO 63351

Tropical Fish Hobbyist
One TFH Plaza
Third and Union Avenues
Neptune City, NJ 07753

The photos on the covers:
Front cover: A variety of guppy (*Poecilia reticulata*).
Inside front cover: A pair of butterfly cichlids (*Papiliochromis ramirezi*)
Inside back cover: A tropical freshwater aquarium with lush vegetatior
Back cover: Cardinal tetras (*Paracheirodon axelrodi*) give colorful acc

Photo credits:
Elias: pages 16, 17, 33, 36, 37; Hansen: page 45; Ifa photo team: pag
Linke: pages 28, 29, 44, 45; Reinhard: front cover; Rössler: inside fro
cover; Schmitt: page 28; Silvestris: page 48; Sommer: pages 18, 24;
Wegler: page 5; Werner: pages 8, 9, 40, 41, 44, 56; Kahl: all other ph

Note of Warning

Electrical appliances used in aquarium maintenance are described in this book. Please be sure to
pay attention to the material on page 10. Otherwise
serious accidents may occur.

Before buying a large aquarium check the floor to
see how much weight it can bear at the spot where
you plan to set up the tank.

Water damage due to broken glass, overflow, or
leaks in the tank cannot always be avoided. Make
sure you are covered by an insurance policy (see
page 10).

Take care that no children (or adults) eat the
aquarium plants. Serious disturbances of their health
may result. Keep all fish medications away from
children.

The spines that loaches have under their eyes
and the fin spines of some catfish species can cause
injuries. Because these puncture wounds can give
rise to allergic reactions, consult a doctor without
delay.

Perfect for Pet Owners!

PET OWNER'S MANUALS

Over 50 illustrations per book (20 or more color photos), 72–80 pp., paperback.

ABYSSINIAN CATS (2864-3)
AFRICAN GRAY PARROTS (3773-1)
AMAZON PARROTS (4035-X)
BANTAMS (3687-5)
BEAGLES (9017-9)
BEEKEEPING (4089-0)
BOSTON TERRIERS (1696-3)
BOXERS (9590-1)
CANARIES (4611-0)
CATS (4442-8)
CHINCHILLAS (4037-6)
CHOW-CHOWS (3952-1)
CICHLIDS (4597-1)
COCKATIELS (4610-2)
COCKER SPANIELS (1478-2)
COCKATOOS (4159-3)
COLLIES (1875-3)
CONURES (4880-6)
DACHSHUNDS (1843-5)
DALMATIANS (4605-6)
DISCUS FISH (4669-2)
DOBERMAN PINSCHERS (9015-2)
DOGS (4822-9)
DOVES (1855-9)
DWARF RABBITS (1352-2)
ENGLISH SPRINGER SPANIELS (1778-1)
FEEDING AND SHELTERING BACKYARD
    BIRDS (4252-2)
FEEDING AND SHELTERING EUROPEAN
    BIRDS (2858-9)
FERRETS (9021-7)
GERBILS (9020-9)
GERMAN SHEPHERDS (2982-8)
GOLDEN RETRIEVERS (9019-5)
GOLDFISH (9016-0)
GOULDIAN FINCHES (4523-8)
GREAT DANES (1418-9)
GUINEA PIGS (4612-9)
GUPPIES, MOLLIES, AND PLATTIES (1497-9)
HAMSTERS (4439-8)
HEDGEHOGS (1141-4)
IRISH SETTERS (4663-3)
KEESHONDEN (1560-6)
KILLIFISH (4475-4)
LABRADOR RETRIEVERS (9018-7)
LHASA APSOS (3950-5)
LIZARDS IN THE TERRARIUM (3925-4)
LONGHAIRED CATS (2803-1)

LONG-TAILED PARAKEETS (1351-4)
LORIES AND LORIKEETS (1567-3)
LOVEBIRDS (9014-4)
MACAWS (4768-0)
MICE (2921-6)
MUTTS (4126-7)
MYNAHS (3688-3)
PARAKEETS (4437-1)
PARROTS (4823-7)
PERSIAN CATS (4405-3)
PIGEONS (4044-9)
POMERANIANS (4670-6)
PONIES (2856-2)
POODLES (2812-0)
POT BELLIES AND OTHER MINIATURE PIGS
    (1356-5)
PUGS (1824-9)
RABBITS (4440-1)
RATS (4535-1)
ROTTWEILERS (4483-5)
SCHNAUZERS (3949-1)
SCOTTISH FOLD CATS (4999-3)
SHAR-PEI (4334-2)
SHEEP (4091-0)
SHETLAND SHEEPDOGS (4264-6)
SHIH TZUS (4524-6)
SIAMESE CATS (4764-8)
SIBERIAN HUSKIES (4265-4)
SMALL DOGS (1951-2)
SNAKES (2813-9)
SPANIELS (2424-9)
TROPICAL FISH (4700-1)
TURTLES (4702-8)
WEST HIGHLAND WHITE TERRIERS (1950-4)
YORKSHIRE TERRIERS (4406-1)
ZEBRA FINCHES (3497-X)

NEW PET HANDBOOKS

Detailed, illustrated profiles (40–60 color photos), 144 pp., paperback.

NEW AQUARIUM FISH HANDBOOK (3682-4)
NEW AUSTRALIAN PARAKEET
    HANDBOOK (4739-7)
NEW BIRD HANDBOOK (4157-7)
NEW CANARY HANDBOOK (4879-2)
NEW CAT HANDBOOK (2922-4)
NEW COCKATIEL HANDBOOK (4201-8)
NEW DOG HANDBOOK (2857-0)
NEW DUCK HANDBOOK (4088-0)
NEW FINCH HANDBOOK (2859-7)

NEW GOAT HANDBOOK (4090-2)
NEW PARAKEET HANDBOOK (2985-2)
NEW PARROT HANDBOOK (3729-4)
NEW RABBIT HANDBOOK (4202-6)
NEW SALTWATER AQUARIUM
    HANDBOOK (4482-7)
NEW SOFTBILL HANDBOOK (4075-9)
NEW TERRIER HANDBOOK (3951-3)

REFERENCE BOOKS

Comprehensive, lavishly illustrated references (60–300 color photos), 136–176 pp., hardcover & paperback.

AQUARIUM FISH (1350-6)
AQUARIUM FISH BREEDING (4474-6)
AQUARIUM FISH SURVIVAL MANUAL
    (9391-7)
AQUARIUM PLANTS MANUAL (1687-4)
BEFORE YOU BUY THAT PUPPY (1750-1)
BEST PET NAME BOOK EVER, THE
    (4258-1)
CARING FOR YOUR SICK CAT (1726-9)
CAT CARE MANUAL (1767-6)
CIVILIZING YOUR PUPPY (4953-5)
COMMUNICATING WITH YOUR DOG
    (4203-4)
COMPLETE BOOK OF BUDGERIGARS
    (6059-8)
COMPLETE BOOK OF CAT CARE (4613-7)
COMPLETE BOOK OF DOG CARE (4158-5)
DOG CARE MANUAL (9163-9)
FEEDING YOUR PET BIRD (1521-5)
GOLDFISH AND ORNAMENTAL CARP
    (9286-4)
GUIDE TO A WELL-BEHAVED CAT
    (1476-6)
GUIDE TO HOME PET GROOMING
    (4298-0)
HEALTHY CAT, HAPPY CAT (9136-1)
HEALTHY DOG, HAPPY DOG (1842-7)
HOP TO IT: A Guide to Training Your Pet
    Rabbit (4551-3)
HORSE CARE MANUAL (1133-3)
HOW TO TALK TO YOUR CAT (1749-8)
HOW TO TEACH YOUR OLD DOG
    NEW TRICKS (4544-0)
LABYRINTH FISH (5635-3)
NONVENOMOUS SNAKES (5632-9)
TROPICAL MARINE FISH
    SURVIVAL MANUAL (9372-0)

Barron's Educational Series, Inc. • 250 Wireless Blvd., Hauppauge, NY 11788
Call toll-free: 1-800-645-3476 • In Canada: Georgetown Book Warehouse
34 Armstrong Ave., Georgetown, Ont. L7G 4R9 • Call toll-free: 1-800-247-7160
ISBN prefix: 0-8120 • Order from your favorite book or pet store

(#62) R 3/96

© Copyright 1990 by Gräfe and Unzer
GmbH, Munich, Germany
The title of the German book is *Das
Aquarium*

Translated from the German by
Kathleen Luft

All inquiries should be addressed to:
Barron's Educational Series, Inc.
250 Wireless Boulevard
Hauppauge, NY 11788

Library of Congress Catalog No. 91-3341

International Standard Book No.
0-8120-4700-1

**Library of Congress Cataloging-in-
Publication Data**

Stadelmann, Peter.
  [Aquarium einrichten und pflegen.
English]
  Tropical fish : setting up and taking care
of aquariums – made easy : expert advice
for new aquarists / Peter Stadelmann ;
consulting editor, Matthew M. Vriends ;
with color photographs by noted aquarium
photographers ; drawings, Fritz W. Köhler.
    p. cm.
  Translation of: Das Aquarium einrichten
und pflegen.
  ISBN 0-8120-4700-1
  1. Aquariums. 2. Tropical fish.
I. Vriends, Matthew M., 1937- II. Title.
SF457.S5913 1991
639.3'4–dc20   91-3341
                                 CIP

Printed in Hong Kong

6 7 8   4900   12 11 10